The Safe Compass

THE SAFE COMPASS AND HOW IT POINTS

SERMONS FOR CHILDREN

ON

THE BIBLE AS OUR SURE GUIDE TO HEAVEN

RICHARD NEWTON

Author of *Heroes of the Early Church,
Heroes of the Reformation, The King's Highway* etc.

SOLID GROUND CHRISTIAN BOOKS
BIRMINGHAM, ALABAMA USA

Solid Ground Christian Books
2090 Columbiana Rd, Suite 2000
Birmingham, AL 35216
205-443-0311
sgcb@charter.net
http://solid-ground-books.com

THE SAFE COMPASS AND HOW IT POINTS
Sermons for Children on the Bible as our Sure Guide to Heaven

Richard Newton (1813-1887)

The Safe Compass from edition by W.P. Nimmo, Hay & Mitchell, Edinburgh, Scotland

Solid Ground Classic Reprints

First printing of new edition March 2006

Cover work by Borgo Design, Tuscaloosa, AL
Contact them at nelbrown@comcast.net

ISBN: 1-59925-059-4

PREFACE.

WHAT a curious thing a compass is! How strangely the little needle trembles on the point of the piece of wire which supports it! How wonderful it is to see that needle always pointing to the north! Who can explain how it is that it always does so? God made it to be always pointing in one direction, and it does just what He wants it to do. This is all we know about it. If you ask a learned man what it is which makes the needle of the compass always point to the north, he will tell you it is *magnetism*. But if you ask him what magnetism is, or how it produces this effect upon the needle, he cannot tell you.

Nobody can explain this. But the compass is not the less useful because none can explain the way in which the needle acts. The compass is one of the most useful things we have. The sailor never could find his way over the sea without it. And those who have to travel over great deserts, or through countries in which there are no roads, always need a compass to show them the direction in which they should go.

PREFACE.

And in going through this world, we are just in this position. The world is like a great desert, or like a country, not indeed without any roads, but full of roads leading in the wrong direction. There is only *one* direction for us to go in, if we wish to pass safely through the world, and reach at last that blessed home which God has prepared for His loving children. And if we desire always to know the direction in which to go in order to reach that home, we must have a compass to take with us in our journey through the world. God has given us the BIBLE to be this *Safe Compass.* It is always pointing towards heaven. And as it points in the right direction, it is always saying to us, ' *This is the way, walk ye in it.*'

Unless we take this compass, and follow its pointings, we cannot get to heaven. The design of this little book is to aid those who are setting out on the great journey of life to make a right use of the compass God has given us. The earnest prayer of the writer is that all his young friends who read these pages may follow the pointings of this *Safe Compass*, and reach at last the blessed world to which it will surely lead them.

CONTENTS.

I
REASONS FOR RESISTING THE ENTICEMENTS OF SINKERS, ... 7
'If sinners entice thee, consent thou not.'—PROV. i. 10.

II.
RELIGION AND RUBIES COMPARED, . . . 22
'She is more precious than rubies.'—PROV. iii. 15.

III.
LESSONS FROM THE ANT, ... 39
'Go to the ant,—consider her ways, and be wise.'—PROV. vi. 6.

IV.
THE HARD WAY, ... 56
'The way of transgressors is hard.'—PROV. xiii. 15.

V.
THE SUNDAY-SCHOOL GARDEN, ... 73
'I am come into my garden.'—CANT. v. 1.

VI.

                                               PAGE

THE WAYS OF DOING GOOD, ... 90

   'Jesus . . . went about doing good.'—ACTS x. 38.

VII.

THE BLESSEDNESS OF GIVING, ... 104

   'Jesus said, It is more blessed to give than to receive.'—
     ACTS xx. 35.

VIII.

GATHERING THE FRAGMENTS: TIME AND KNOW-
   LEDGE, ... 118

   'Gather up the fragments . . . that nothing be lost.'—
     JOHN vi. 12.

IX.

GATHERING THE FRAGMENTS: MONEY AND USE-
   FULNESS, ... 133

   'Gather up the fragments . . . that nothing be lost.'—
     JOHN vi. 12.

X.

THE BEST HELPER, ... 147

   'I will help thee.'—ISAIAH xli. 10.

THE SAFE COMPASS.

I.

Reasons for Resisting the Enticements of Sinners.

'*If sinners entice thee, consent thou not.*'—Prov. i. 10.

IF I should ask you, Who are meant by sinners? you would, perhaps, give me a good many answers, and of different kinds. One would say, sinners are persons that curse and swear. Another would say, thieves and robbers are meant by sinners. Another would say, murderers are sinners. Another would say, sinners mean those who get drunk and break the Sabbath. And so on. All these answers would be correct, for it is true that all the different persons named are sinners. But none of these would be the proper answer, or the best answer to give to the question—who are meant by sinners? When God speaks about sinners in the Bible, He does not mean *only* those persons who swear, or steal, or commit murder, or do such dreadful things, but he means *all persons who are not true Christians*. All men and women, all boys and girls whose hearts have not been changed, and who do not love the Saviour, are sinners in God's sight. Whenever we read about 'sinners' in the Bible, these are the persons intended. This is the meaning of the word 'sinners' in our text. Do you know who wrote the book of Proverbs? Solomon. He was the great king of Israel, the wisest man, excepting our blessed Saviour, who ever lived. Now let us see what Solomon speaks of sinners as doing in our text. He says, 'If sinners *entice* thee.' What does it mean to entice a person? It means to persuade or coax him to commit sin, or to do something wrong. If you are trying to get a person to do right, we never call it *enticing* him. It is only when people are trying to make others do wrong, that we use the word *entice*.

The meaning of the text then is,—if persons who are not Christians, who don't love Jesus, try to persuade you to do wrong, don't mind them. For instance— suppose you are on your way to Sunday-school some bright, beautiful Sunday morning. At the corner of the street you meet some young friends. One of them says to you, 'Good morning, John, where are you going?' You answer, 'I am going to Sunday-school. Where are *you* going?' He says—

'Oh, we're going out to spend the day at Fairmount Park. We've got our dinner in that basket. You'd better come along, John, we're going to have lots of fun.' Now what would your friend be doing? He would be a *sinner enticing* you to break the fourth commandment.

Suppose you are spending your summer vacation. One fine afternoon you go out to play in the woods. Adjoining the woods is an apple orchard. Before you go, your mother says to you, 'Well, Johnny, I hope you'll have a nice time in the woods. But, remember, you are not to go into the orchard on any account, or to take any of the fruit there. Do you hear?'

'Yes, mother.'

But it's a warm afternoon. After a while some of the boys start for the orchard, and begin eating the apples. But you remember what your mother said, and go on with your play.

Presently, one of the boys calls out to you:
'Halloo, John, don't you want some apples?'
'No,' you answer very promptly; 'mother told me not to take any, and I don't intend to.'
'We're not going to climb up the trees,' he says, 'but only to take some of those lying on the ground. It won't do any harm to take these. They are so ripe and juicy! Just come over and taste them.'

What would that boy be doing? He would be a sinner *enticing* you to break the fifth commandment, by disobeying your mother. And so, whenever anybody tries to persuade you to commit sin,—to lie, or swear, or break the Sabbath, or disobey your parents, or to do anything, no matter what, which the Bible says you must not do,—that person is a *sinner* trying to *entice* you. And here, in the text, God tells you what to do in all such cases. He says, 'If sinners entice thee, consent thou *not.*' Don't yield to their enticements. Don't let them persuade you to join them in sin. This is the great lesson we should learn from our text.

I pray God to write this text on every heart here this afternoon. Oh, how many sorrows and troubles it will save you from, if you will only remember this text, and mind it when 'sinners entice' you!

I wish now to speak of *three* reasons why we should not consent when sinners entice us.

The first reason is, because when we begin to sin it's hard to stop.

There was a boy whose name was Frank. He was in the orchard on the side of a hill. His father was in the yard adjoining the orchard, at the foot of the hill. He called to him, 'Frank, come here.'

'Yes, sir,' said Frank, and started to run at full speed down the hill. He ran ever so far past his father, towards the house.

'Frank, come here, I say; didn't you hear me call?' asked his father.

'Yes, sir,' said Frank.

'Well, then, what made you run past me?'

'Oh!' said Frank, '*I got started and couldn't stop.*'

This is just the way in which people fall into sin. 'Sinners entice them,' and they consent. 'They get running and can't stop.'

'I went a short time ago,' said a gentleman to a friend, 'to the jail, to see a young man who had once been a Sunday-school scholar. The keeper took a large bunch of keys, and led us through the long, gloomy halls, unlocking one door after another, until at length he opened the door of the room in which sat the young man we had come to see. The walls of the room were of coarse stone, the floor of thick plank, and before the windows were strong iron bars.

'Without, all was beautiful: the green fields, the sweet flowers, and the singing birds were as lovely as ever, but this young man could enjoy none of them; no, never could he look on them again, for he was condemned to death. He had killed a man, and now he himself was to die. Think of it,—only twenty years old, and yet a murderer!

'I sat down beside him and talked with him. "Oh!" said he, as the tears rolled down his cheeks, "to think that I should come to this! I didn't mean to do it, but I was drunk; then I got angry, and before I knew what I was about, I killed him. Oh, if I had only minded my mother, and listened to my Sunday-school teacher, I never should have come to this; I never should have been here!"'

This young man 'got started and couldn't stop.' When 'sinners enticed him' to break the Sabbath, to disobey his mother, to drink and gamble, he ought not to have consented. It would have been easy for him to take his stand then; but when he once began to sin, like a stone thrown down the side of a mountain, he found it hard to stop.

As the gentleman left him, he said: 'Will you pray

for me, sir? And oh! tell boys everywhere to mind their mothers, and keep away from bad companions.'

Think of this young man whenever you read or hear the words of the text: 'If sinners entice thee, consent thou not.'

The Arabs have a fable about *The Miller and the Camel*, which illustrates very well the importance of minding this text. The fable says, that one day in winter the miller was sleeping in his house when he was awakened by a noise. On looking up he saw a camel who had thrust his nose through the window of the room.

'It's very cold out here,' said the camel; 'please let me just put my nose into your room to get a little warmed.' 'Very well,' said the miller. After a while the camel asked leave to put his neck in; and then he begged to have his forefeet in the room; and so he kept on, by little and little, until at last he crowded in his whole body.

Then he began to walk about the room, and knock things over, and do just as he pleased. The miller soon found him so rude and troublesome that the room was not large enough for them both. He began to complain to the camel of the trouble he was giving him, and told him to go out. 'If you don't like the room, you can leave it whenever you choose,' said the camel; 'as for myself, I am very comfortable, and intend to stay where I am.'

This is just the way it is with sin. It comes knocking at our hearts, and begs for entrance a little way. As the old proverb says, 'if you give it an inch, it will take an ell.' It goes on increasing its power, step by step, until it becomes master in the soul. It would have been easy enough for the miller to have kept the camel out when he had only his nose in the window; but after he got his whole body into the room, it was hard work to get him out. So when sin or sinners entice us, we should not consent. We should guard against the first beginning of it. Don't let its nose get in at the window, and then its body will never get into the room. The

Bible tells us to flee from the *appearance* of evil. Let us resolve to do this; and above all, let us pray for the help of the Holy Spirit, that by His grace we may be able to 'keep our hearts with all diligence,' and guard against the entrance of anything that may, as one of our Collects says, 'assault or hurt the soul.' 'If sinners entice thee, consent thou not.' The first reason why we should not consent is, *that when we begin to sin it's hard to stop.*

But the second reason why we ought not to consent to sin is, because it is DANGEROUS.

Here is a long train of carriages on a railway. They are crowded with passengers, and are flying pleasantly along at full speed. Now they come to where the track goes along near a high bank. Here some wicked person has placed a heavy log of wood across the track. The train comes thundering on. The engineer does not see the log. Presently the engine comes up against it with a tremendous crash. It is thrown off the track. It drags the train after it. One after another the carriages roll down the bank. Many of them are broken to pieces. A dreadful scene of confusion follows. Ten or fifteen of the passengers are killed, and great numbers of them wounded. All this loss and misery is produced by the log that was laid across that track. Was it not a very dangerous thing to place that log there? Yes; for it threw that train of carriages off the track and occasioned all that mischief.

Now, sin is dangerous in just the same way. God's commandments are the path of duty He has prepared for us to walk in—the track on which He would have us run. But sin, like the log against which the engine ran, throws us off the track of duty, and causes great harm. Look at Adam and Eve in the garden of Eden. They were like the first two in a long train of carriages. When Satan *enticed* them to sin, he laid a log on their track. When they consented to sin they ran against that log. This threw *them* off the track, and every carriage in the long, long train that came after them. All the war, and misery, and suffering, and death which have filled the world since then, have been the effect of throwing that train off the track. Jesus has been occupied nearly 6,000 years in trying to get that train on the track again. It is not on yet, but He is sure to get it on at last. This shows us what a dangerous thing it is to consent to sin.

Not long ago some workmen were engaged in building a large brick tower, which was to be carried up very high. The master builder was very particular in charging the masons to lay every brick with the greatest care, especially in the first courses, or rows, which had to bear the weight of all the rest of the building. However, one of the workmen did not mind what had been told him. In laying a corner he very carelessly left one of the bricks a little crooked, out of the line; or, as the masons call it, 'not plumb.' Well, you may say, 'It was only *one single brick* in a great pile of them. What difference does it make if that was not exactly straight?' You will see directly. The work went on. Nobody noticed that there was one brick wrong. But as each new course of bricks was kept in a line with those already laid, the tower was not put up exactly straight, and the higher they built it the more insecure it became. One day, when the tower had been carried up about fifty feet, a tremendous crash was heard. The building had fallen to the ground, burying the workmen in the ruins. All the previous work was lost, the materials were wasted; and worse than this, valuable lives were sacrificed, and all because *one brick had been laid wrong* at the start. The workman who carelessly laid that brick wrong, little thought what a dangerous thing he was doing, and what terrible harm would result from his neglect. My dear young friends, you are now building up your character. In the habits you now form you are laying the foundation of that character. One bad habit, one brick laid wrong *now*, may ruin your character by and by. Remember what you are doing, and see that *every brick* is kept *straight.* 'If sinners entice thee, consent thou not,' because it is dangerous.

But this part of our subject is so important, that I must give you another illustration of the *danger* of consenting to sin before we leave it.

There was a minister once who had a bright, beautiful boy named James. He was his only child. It was on a clear, calm, lovely Sabbath morning in June that the event took place of which I am about to tell you. The cherries were ripe, and the green leaves which were around them made them appear very nice and tempting. James's father was about to leave home to go to church. Knowing that his son sometimes acted very improperly when he was away, he was afraid that he might be tempted to disobey his father and break the Sabbath in order to get the cherries. So, before he started, he called James to him, and said, 'My son, do you know what day this is?'

'Yes, sir; it's the Sabbath day.'

'Can you wait until to-morrow for the cherries, which are ripe?'

'Yes, sir,' answered James.

'Now remember, my dear boy, that this is God's day. Don't go near that tree. Don't forget your father's command.'

'No, sir,' said he.

After his father had disappeared over the hill, and his nurse was engaged in another part of the house, he took his stand at the open window, and stood gazing at the bright, beautiful fruit, as they hung upon the tree, so ripe and juicy. Perhaps you are ready to say, that 'there were no sinners there to tempt James.' Yes, there was. Satan was there, that old father of sin and sinners. He is the greatest of all enticers. He came up to James, unseen, and whispered in his ear, 'Don't they look ripe? Wouldn't it be nice to have a few? What's to hinder? The nurse is away. Nobody will see you. Your father will never know it. Why not go and get a few?' Thus

Satan enticed James. *And James consented.* After he had filled his *eye* and his *heart* with the cherries, he resolved to fill his *hands* and his *mouth.* He stole quietly out of the house, and climbed up the tree. He had eaten as many as he wanted then, and was plucking some to put in his pocket, when the door of the house opened suddenly. This frightened him. He missed his hold, and fell some twelve feet to the ground. The servant ran to pick him up, and carry him into the house. But his neck was broken, and there lay the young Sabbath-breaker, *dead!* He had died in the very act of breaking two of God's commandments at once, the fourth and the fifth.

At noon his father returned. He found his little boy dead. How must he have felt? Ah! if we had been there, we would have seen him wringing his hands in sorrow, while he took up David's lamentation over Absalom, and said: 'My son! my son! would God that I had died for thee! O James, my son! my son!'

'If sinners entice thee, consent thou not.' Don't do it, because *it is dangerous.*

The third reason why we should not consent to sin is, because it is DISGRACEFUL.

Sin is disgraceful in two ways: It is disgraceful in the *looks it gives us,* and in the *company* into which it brings us. The looks it gives us; why, you ask, What has sin to do with our looks? I tell you, it has a great deal to do with our looks.

I suppose you have all seen a gutta-percha face? And I dare say you have amused yourself in pinching it one way, and pulling it another, and seeing what different expressions it will put on. But when you stop pulling or pinching it, it returns to the same face that it was before.

Now, your faces are softer than gutta-percha, and they are full of little strings called muscles. These muscles, or strings, are pulled one way or pulled another, just according to your feelings. Sometimes you feel grieved or sad, and the little muscles pull your face into a very doleful expression. The moment anybody looks at you they know something is troubling you, and you feel sorrowful. But if you see a funny picture, or if something happens to make you feel merry and glad, the little muscles pull your face into smiles and dimples, and you look just ready to burst out into a broad laugh.

But when we commit sin, wicked feelings are at work pulling these strings. Anger pulls one set of strings, and then you know what a disagreeable look the face puts on in a moment! Pride pulls another set of these strings, and so does vanity, or envy, or deceit, or discontent; and each of these brings its own peculiar look or expression over the face. And the worst thing about it is, that if these strings are pulled too often the face will not return to what it was before, but the strings will become stiff, like wires, and the face will keep wearing the ugly look it put on all the time. By giving way to sin, or indulging their bad feelings, some people get their faces worked up to such a dreadful look, that when you meet one of them in the street, the moment you see him you can tell what his character is.

A face that was very lovely when it was that of a child, if it has the passion of anger often pulling at it, will get at last to wear all the time a sullen, cross, dissatisfied look. Or if a man has learned to love money better than anything else, and to hoard it up for its own sake, this will pull a set of strings that will fix a close, mean, grasping look upon his face, so that as you pass him you will be ready to say, 'There goes a miser.' Or if one learns to lie and steal, his face will show it by and by; it will be impossible for him to put on an honest, truthful look.

You know, my dear children, the Bible tells us that sin is a reproach or a disgrace, and if we consent to it, or give way to it, it will pull those strings in our faces that will make our very looks to be disgraceful. Don't let anger, or pride, or passion, get hold of the strings, or they will make you appear so ugly that no one will like to look at you. But let love, and gentleness, and goodwill, and truth, and honesty, have hold of the strings, and they will make your faces beautiful and lovely.

Did you ever hear the story of the *Two Portraits?* It comes in so nicely to illustrate this part of our subject that I must tell it here.

An Italian painter once wanted to get a painting that would do to represent the head and face of an angel. One day, as he was passing through the streets, he saw a little child whose face was the brightest, the sweetest, and the most beautiful he had ever seen. He said to himself, 'That is just what I want.' He asked permission to paint a likeness of the head and face of that child. It was granted. He finished it, and hung it up in his study. Everybody admired it. The sweet, gentle look of that face seemed like an angel's look. He often gazed upon it when he was disturbed or troubled, and it seemed to soothe him and do him good. He used to say that he would like to paint another head, to be the very opposite of this—as unlike it, in every respect, as possible. Then he would have the two portraits to hang side by side—the one, as the head of an angel; the other, as the head of a fiend; the one to represent heaven, the other to represent hell. But many years passed away before he found any one who looked horrible enough to be the subject for the second picture. At length, in a distant land, he was once visiting a prison. There he saw a man whose appearance was the most dreadful he had ever seen. His face had the fierce, haggard look of a fiend, with glaring eyes, and cheeks deeply marked with lust and crime. The moment he saw the man he said to himself, 'This will do for my second portrait.' He painted a picture of this loathsome face to hang beside that beautiful angel head, which had been in his study so long. And when they hung there side by side, oh how great the contrast between them was! The one looked, for all the world, like the face of an angel, and the other like the face of a fiend. But when the painter came to inquire into the history of the prisoner, you may judge what his surprise was, when he found this hideous-looking man was the very same person whose face, when a child, he had taken, from which to paint his portrait of an angel. And now that face was so changed, that he painted his portrait of a fiend from it. And what had made this surprising change? One little word of three letters—*sin*. I said that sin was disgraceful in the looks it gives us. Here you see how true this is!

But sin is *disgraceful also in the company to which it brings us.* When Jesus was on earth He said, 'Whosoever committeth sin is the *servant* of sin.' Now, so far as we know, Satan was the first sinner. He is the author, or father of sin. And if we are the servants of sin, we must be the servants of Satan also. But can there be any greater disgrace than this? You know that in some cities, when men have committed great crimes for which they are condemned to the penitentiary, they are obliged to wear a particular kind of prison dress. Then they are chained together in gangs of three or four, and compelled to sweep the streets, and do other such like work for the city authorities. Now, suppose you had a young friend about 18 or 19 years old. We may call him Charles Jackson. He has had a good education. His parents are well off, and very respectable. His father is an eminent physician in this city. But Charles was a bad boy. He gave his parents a great deal of trouble, and several years ago he ran away from home. And suppose that one day you are walking through the streets of one of those cities where the prisoners, in chains, are made to act as scavengers. As you go along you pass one of those chain-gangs of prisoners. You look up in passing, and there, to your surprise and sorrow, you see, chained in between criminals, your old friend Charles Jackson! Oh, how shocked you are! You say to yourself, what a disgrace to be found in such company! *Sin* brought that disgrace upon Charles.

Now do you know that Satan and the wicked spirits with him are God's chain-gang prisoners. The Bible tells us that they are 'reserved,' or kept, 'in *everlasting chains* under darkness' (Jude 6). Or, as it calls them in another place, 'in *chains of darkness*.' They are God's prisoners in chains. And all who consent to sin are bound in the same gang with them. And if we remain in the company of Satan here, in this life, we must share the wages which he will receive at last, and be shut up in company with him for ever. There is one passage in the Bible which speaks about this, and it is enough to make one's blood run cold just to read it or hear it. It is the 25th chapter of Matthew and 41st verse. Here Jesus is describing the solemn scenes of the judgment day. He is seated on His glorious throne. The holy angels are about Him. All nations are gathered before Him. On His right hand stand the righteous, *i.e.* all who have loved and served Him. He smiles on them and says, 'Come, ye blessed children of my Father, receive the kingdom prepared for you from the foundation of the world.' On His left hand stand the wicked, *i.e.* all who have consented to sin and served Satan. He turns to them with an awful frown, and says, 'Depart, ye cursed, into everlasting fire, *prepared for the devil* and his angels!' Dreadful, dreadful words! If the *fire* was prepared for the devil and his angels, the *place* was prepared for them too. Only think of being shut up in the company of all wicked angels and men for ever! What a disgrace! The third reason why we should not consent to sin is that it is *disgraceful*.

Here, then, we have three good reasons why we should not consent to sin. *The first is, because when we begin it is hard to stop; the second is, because it is dangerous; and the third, because it is disgraceful.*

In conclusion, my dear children, there are two things we ought all of us to do. *We ought to get rid of the sins we have committed.* This is one thing. We are all sinners. Every one of us has committed sin. The great thing is to get rid of it. Now there is only *One Person* in all the universe who can take away sin. This is Jesus. He came, the Bible tells us, 'to put away sin by the sacrifice of Himself.' He was nailed to the cross, and shed His precious blood for this purpose. Hence the Bible tells us that 'the blood of Jesus Christ cleanseth from all sin.' If we are truly sorry for our sins, and pray God for *His sake* to pardon our sins, they will be all forgiven. He will blot them out of His book of remembrance, and they will never be mentioned any more. This is one thing we ought to do. *Get rid of the sins we have committed.*

And then there is another thing we ought to do, and *that is, to try and keep from sinning any more.*

Said a boy to his sister one day, 'I want the spirit to look sin right in the face when it comes to me, and say, Begone.'

'Yes, brother,' said his sister, 'and one thing more you want: you want God's spectacles to see sin and know it when it comes, for it doesn't always show its colours.'

I suppose by 'God's spectacles' this good girl meant the Bible. This helps us to see things as God sees them, just as though we were looking at them through His spectacles. There is nothing like the Bible to show us what sin is. And then, while it shows us what is sin, it shows us how to deal with it. 'If sinners entice thee, consent thou not.' Take your stand at once. Don't trifle with it. The moment it appears resist it.

In front of my house there are two young shade trees, or rather, one in front of my house and the other in front of my next-door neighbour's house. Last spring they both came out in leaf beautifully. They looked very green and flourishing. After a while the worms appeared, —those long, black, ugly-looking creatures that play such havoc with our shade trees every spring. Well, one day, when I was going out of the house, I stopped a moment to look at the tree, and found the worms had fairly got possession of it, and were likely, in a few days, to eat up all the leaves. I shook my head and said, 'Ah! my gentlemen, this'll never do.' So I went in and got a chair to stand upon, and taking a cane in my hand, I went to work and knocked off and killed every worm that was on the tree. That saved the tree. It has been growing nicely all the summer. But my neighbour let the worms alone on his tree. The consequence was that they ate up every particle of leaf that was on it. Then the tree died, and every time I look at its bare, black, dismal-looking, dead branches, it teaches me a lesson. It seems to tell me the importance of resisting sin as soon as it appears. What the worms were to that tree, sins are to your soul. Oh! pray God to give you grace to see your sins as soon as they appear, and to try to get rid of them at once.

'If sinners entice thee, consent thou not.'

II.

Religion and Rubies Compared.

'*She is more precious than rubies.*'—Prov. iii. 15.

SOLOMON is speaking of *religion* here. He calls it wisdom. Wisdom is always represented as a female. The first word in the text, the pronoun *she*, means religion. Suppose, now, that we put this word in place of the pronoun she, and then the verse will read in this way, 'Religion is more precious than rubies.'

A ruby is a beautiful gem. It is a precious stone of a bright rose or blood-red colour. If you look at a ruby when the sunlight is on it, you will see it shining and sparkling in the most beautiful manner. Among precious stones the ruby is reckoned the most valuable next to the diamond. And because it is considered so valuable, religion is here compared to it. Solomon was a good judge both of rubies and of religion. He was the richest man on the earth at the time in which he lived. He had gold and silver almost without any end. He had all kinds of jewels and precious stones. Among these, no doubt, he had a great many rubies. He knew how much they were worth, and what they were good for. And then Solomon was a pious man. He knew very well how much religion was worth. He knew what it was good for. So that we know he understood what he was speaking about when he wrote the words of which

RELIGION AND RUBIES COMPARED. 23

we are now thinking. But Solomon was not speaking for himself when he used these words. 'A greater than Solomon is here.' It is God who is here speaking through him. Solomon was one of those 'holy men of old' whom the Holy Ghost employed to write the Bible. What those men said was not their own words, but God's. 'They spake as they were moved by the Holy Ghost.' It is God, then, who is here speaking of religion, and says, 'She is more precious than rubies.' God knows how much rubies are worth, for He made them all. And God knows how much religion is worth, for He is the Author of it. Now here, you see, we have two things to examine or compare together—*religion and rubies*. This is the subject of our sermon this afternoon. When you go home from church to-day, if anybody asks you what was the sermon about, you can say it was about *religion and rubies compared.*

'*She is more precious than rubies.*'

Now, the question we have to answer is, in what way is religion more precious than rubies? I wish to speak of *five* ways in which this is so.

And in the first place, religion is more precious than rubies in the WAY OF INSTRUCTION.

A ruby is a very beautiful thing to look at. It glitters and sparkles in such a way that you can't help admiring it. But what can a ruby teach you? What instruction can it give you? Suppose that you have one of the largest and most valuable rubies that the world contains, but, at the same time, that you have no Bible. Suppose also, that you have never seen or heard of a Bible. You have never had a single lesson from it. You are entirely ignorant of all the great things which the Bible teaches. Now, how much could you learn about those things from your ruby? You look upon this beautiful world around you,—the fields, the woods, the mountains, the hills, the plains, the valleys, the rivers, and springs that run among the hills,—the sun as it shines by day, and the moon and the stars as they shine by night,—and you want to know who made them all. And can your ruby tell you? Oh, no! But here religion comes with her Bible. Can she tell you? Yes, indeed. She opens the first chapter of this wonderful book and reads, 'In the beginning *God* created the heavens and the earth.' You look at yourself. What a wonderful creature you are! How strangely your body is made, with its eyes, and ears, and hands, and feet, and heart, and lungs! And then the *soul* that dwells in this moving house; the soul that thinks, and feels, and loves, and hates,—who made it and put it in this curious body? The ruby cannot tell you anything about it. But religion can tell you. She opens her wondrous book again and reads, 'The Lord God formed man out of the dust of the ground, and breathed into his nostrils the breath of life, and man became a living soul.'

You have a dear little brother whom you love very much. He is taken sick. The doctor comes to see him—but can't cure him. He dies. You see him put into the coffin. The lid is screwed down upon him. Then comes the funeral. You go to the grave-yard. The coffin is lowered into the grave. You lean over and look down. How cold and damp it seems! Now the men shovel in the earth, and your little brother is hidden from your sight. You want to know what has become of him. And can your ruby tell you? No. But here is religion with her Bible. She opens it and reads, 'The dust,' *i.e.* the body, 'shall return to the earth as it was; and the spirit shall return unto God who gave it.'— Eccles. xii. 7.

But you have seen the flowers in the garden all wither and die when winter came; yet on the return of spring, they start up and grow again. You have seen the little worm weave a sort of coffin around itself. In this it has lain all winter, as if dead. But in spring that little coffin opens, and instead of the crawling worm, out comes a beautiful butterfly. Now, as you stand by your little brother's grave, you want to know whether he will live

RELIGION AND RUBIES COMPARED.

again like the flowers, or whether his coffin will open and he will come out again as much changed as the worm was when turned into a butterfly. Oh, how anxious you are to know this! Well, ask your beautiful ruby. Can it give you any answer? Not a word. But here is religion with her Bible. Ask her. She opens the Bible and reads, 'Thy brother shall rise again.'— John xi. 23. 'The hour is coming in which all that are in the graves shall hear the voice of the Son of Man and shall come forth.'—John v. 28.

You have heard that God made you, and the world, and all things. You know that He is very powerful, and can do whatever He desires. But you wish to know what sort of a God He is. Is He kind, and loving, and gentle? or is He angry, and fierce, and cruel? These are questions which your ruby can't answer. But ask religion about them. She opens her Bible and reads, 'God is love.'—1 John iv. 8. 'The Lord is good unto all, and His tender mercies are over all His works.'— Ps. cxlv. 9. And now suppose that you are going to die yourself. You feel that you are a sinner, and are afraid to die. You want to know how your sins can be pardoned, so that you may go to heaven when you die. Can your ruby tell you? No. But you ask religion. She opens her Bible and reads, 'The blood of Jesus Christ His Son cleanseth from all sin.'—1 John i. 7. 'Believe on the Lord Jesus Christ and thou shalt be saved.'—Acts xvi. 31.

A little girl, named Mary, had been going to Sunday school for some time. She was only about seven or eight years old. But she had learned enough to know that she was a sinner, and that Jesus was the only Saviour. She loved Him, and prayed to Him every day. Mary's parents never went to church, and never read the Bible. They were careless, wicked people, who never thought about God or heaven. One night Mary's father was taken suddenly ill. His illness was very alarming. The poor man saw death staring him in the face. He felt that he was a sinner, and not prepared to die. He asked his wife to pray for him. She said she didn't know how to pray. 'Oh, what shall I do?' he exclaimed, 'how can I die with all my sins upon me?'

'Mary has learned a great deal about the Bible at Sunday-school,' said his wife; 'suppose I call her. Perhaps she can tell you something that will comfort you.'

'Call her at once,' said he.

Mary was called, out of her sleep, to the bedside of her dying father. 'Mary, my child,' said the poor man, 'I'm going to die; but I feel that I'm a great sinner. Can you tell me how a sinner like me can be saved?'

'Oh yes, father,' said Mary, 'Jesus Christ came into the world to save sinners.'

'But how does He save sinners? and will He save such a great sinner as I am?'

'Jesus says, in the Bible,' replied Mary, '"Come unto me, all ye that labour and are heavy laden, and I will give you rest." "God so loved the world that He gave His only begotten Son, that whosoever believeth in Him should not perish, but have everlasting life." "Him that cometh unto me I will in no wise cast out."'

'Does the Bible say all that, Mary?' asked the dying man with great earnestness.

'Yes,' said Mary; 'those are the very words I learned in Sunday-school.'

Then he asked Mary to kneel down and pray for him. So she kneeled down and prayed that God would have mercy on her dear father; that he would pardon his sins, and save his soul, for Jesus' sake.

In the morning, when Mary woke up, her father was dead. But he died believing the words that Mary had told him from the Bible, and he found peace in believing them. But suppose that Mary had taken a handful of rubies to her dying father, instead of the instructions she gave him from the Bible, would they have done him any good? None at all. Well, then, you see that religion is more precious than rubies in the *way of instruction.*

The second way in which it is more precious is in the WAY OF HELP.

I mean by this, that religion will do a great deal more to help us under the troubles that we have to meet with in life, than rubies can do. I don't think I can illustrate this part of our subject better than by telling you about a poor boy, so that you can see what religion did to help him under his difficulties.

A minister of the gospel, after an absence of several years, returned to spend a Sabbath at a town in England where he had formerly been settled. After the services were over, a widow woman knocked at the door of the vestry-room, and desired to see him. ' Don't you remember me, sir?' she asked.

'No, I do not,' said he.

'Don't you remember my John? He used to be in the Sunday school.'

'I can't say that I do,' answered the minister.

'O sir,' said the old woman, '*my John* is the *best John in the world;* and I thought I would like to tell you about him.'

The minister said he would be glad to hear what she had to say; and then she told her story as follows:

'After you left us, sir, my husband died, and we became very poor, indeed we were almost starving. One day John said to me, "Mother, dear, we can't starve, and there is no work to be got; let me go to sea for a time, and try to earn some money for you." I was very unwilling to part from him; but times were bad, and as he seemed so anxious about it, I gave him a parting kiss and prayer, and with his Bible in his pocket, and a bundle in his hand, he set off to the nearest seaport town, to try and get a situation on board a ship. He went from vessel to vessel among the docks, for several days, but could not get a situation. At last, when he was almost discouraged, he saw the captain of a ship passing by. "Don't you want a boy, sir?" said John. "Why, that's the very thing I'm looking for," said the captain. "Do then, sir, take me." "Well, where is your character?" "Nobody knows me here, sir," said John. "But in my own parish I could get a character in a minute." "I can't take you without a character." The captain was turning away when John thought of his Bible, and opening it in an instant, he said, "How will that do, sir?" The captain read the following:

PRESENTED TO

John Reynolds

FOR HIS GOOD BEHAVIOUR IN SUNDAY SCHOOL.

"That'll do, my boy," said the captain, "come along." Accordingly John was shipped in a merchant vessel bound for St. Petersburg. During the voyage a dreadful storm arose. The wind blew a hurricane, and every one expected the vessel to be lost. The sailors had done all they could, and were waiting to see the end. Then John took out his Bible, and in a loud, solemn voice, read out the 51st Psalm. While he was doing this, one after another, the sailors first and then the officers, gathered round him. When he had done reading, he kneeled down and prayed very earnestly that God would make the storm to cease, and spare their lives. God heard that prayer, and soon after the storm began to abate. The captain acknowledged that John's prayers had saved the ship, and promised him a holiday when they got to St. Petersburg.

'He kept his word, and while the ship was lying there, he gave John the promised holiday. Boy-like, John went to the palace of the emperor to see all the great people go to court. As he stood in wonder, gazing on carriage after carriage passing by, something dropped at his feet. It was a bracelet, sparkling with jewels, which had dropped from a lady's hand. John picked it up, and called aloud for the coachman to stop, but in vain; the crowd and the noise prevented John from being noticed, and he returned to the ship with the bracelet. "You're a lucky fellow," said the captain; "why, these are diamonds." "Yes, sir; but they are *not mine.*" "How did you get them?" "I picked them up, and called to the driver to stop; but he drove on, and didn't hear me." "Then you did all you could under the circumstances, and they are clearly yours." "No, captain; they are not mine," said John. "You foolish fellow," said the captain, "let me have the diamonds, and when we get back to London I'll sell them for you, and they'll fetch lots of money." "That may be, sir; but they are *not mine;* and suppose, captain, we should have another storm as we go home, what then?" "Ay, ay, Jack," said the captain, "I didn't think of that! Well, we must try and find the owner." This was done. The lady gave Jack a sum of money as a reward for his honesty. This money, at the advice of the captain, was laid out in skins and hides. When these were sold on their return, John left the ship, after his first voyage, with eighty pounds in his pocket. He came straight home to his native village. He found me in the workhouse. He took me out and rented a nice little cottage for me, and there he has supported me ever since. He is the captain of a ship now; but he never forgets his old mother. I tell you, sir,' said she, ending as she began, '*my John's the best John in the world.*'

The minister thought she had good reason to think so. But just see how religion helped this boy under his troubles, in a way in which the best ruby in the world never could have done. It was religion that taught John to love and honour his mother, and do all that he could to help and comfort her. It was religion which gave him that Bible with the recommendation in it, and this secured him a situation. It was religion which taught him to read that Bible for comfort in the storm and to pray to God for help, when the officers and men could no longer help themselves. It was religion that saved that ship, and all on board, from destruction. It was religion that kept John from acting dishonestly about the bracelet he had found. That was the turning-point of his history. If he had done wrong then he probably never would have succeeded as he afterwards did. It was religion which built up for John the good character he possessed, and secured him his success in life. But what could rubies have done in the place of religion on any of these occasions? And so you see, clearly enough, that religion is better, *i.e.* 'more precious than rubies' in the way of help.

But religion is more precious than rubies in the WAY OF COMFORT.

It is surprising to find in how many different ways people are afflicted and troubled in this world. But whatever the trouble is to which those who love Jesus, and are truly religious, are exposed, they find that their religion gives them such comfort as no gold or silver or jewels could ever give them.

There was a good man once who was very rich. He had so much money, and so many good things, that one of his Christian friends asked him one day if he was not afraid of forgetting God, and thinking too much of his money. His answer was, 'No; for I enjoy God in all things.' After a while he lost all his property, and was reduced almost to beggary. His old friend was afraid this would be too much for him, and asked him if his great losses did not make him feel very unhappy? But with a cheerful smile he answered, 'No; for now I *enjoy all things in God.*' Ah! if rich people would learn to enjoy *God in all things*, their riches would never do them any harm. And if the poor would learn to enjoy *all things in God*, they would always be happy even in their poverty. Religion can give people comfort under trials when no rubies, or jewels of any kind, could afford them any pleasure.

Some time ago there was a Brahmin, in India, who was very rich. He owned many houses and extensive lands. He had a beautiful wife and numerous children. From conversation with a missionary, and from reading the New Testament, he was led to become a Christian. But when he was baptized, according to the custom of that country, all his friends and relations forsook him. He was disowned by them all. Not one of them would speak to him, or have anything to do with him. All his property, too, was taken from him. He was left without a penny, and was obliged to work for his own living. One day a British officer, who was a Christian himself, and knew what this man had suffered by becoming a Christian, asked him how he bore his sorrows, and if he was supported under them. 'Ah!' said he, 'I am often asked that. But nobody asks me how I bear my joys. The Lord Jesus sought me out and found me, a poor, stray sheep in the wilderness. He brought me to His fold, and fills me with joy unspeakable and full of glory.' What could rubies do to make a man happy under such circumstances? But religion gave this man such comfort that, like Paul of old, when he had endured ' the loss of all things' earthly, he considered it 'a *gain*, that he might win Christ.'

There was a poor woman in England whose name was Harriet Stoneman. She was afflicted for *thirty-nine years* with a most distressing disease. Her sufferings at times were dreadful. It was just as if her bones were being ground to pieces, or burnt up in her body. At first she was the most miserable and unhappy creature that you can imagine. But after a while she became a Christian, and learned to love Jesus. Then she was a *new creature* indeed. Her religion did not cure her disease, or take away her pains; but, oh, it gave her wonderful support and comfort under them. Great as her sufferings were, she never murmured or complained, but always seemed cheerful and happy. She always had some pleasant word to speak of Jesus, and the joy she found in Him.

Three shillings a week was all she had for her support. Yet out of this small sum for *twenty-eight* years she regularly laid by a penny for the missionary cause. And notwithstanding her sufferings, she used to be constantly writing letters and sending tracts to people, to try and do them good. Now, suppose this woman had had a house full of rubies and gems given to her, what could they have done to comfort her? Nothing at all. But in her greatest distress she found real comfort in her religion.

Let us take one more illustration of this part of our subject. Several years ago a large steamer, called the *Austria*, caught fire at sea in going from England to America. She had a great number of passengers on board. Every effort was made to put out the fire, but in vain. They couldn't get at the engine to stop it, and the progress of the vessel through the water only fanned the flames, and made the fire burn the faster. The only prospect before the passengers was a choice between two ways of dying. They must either jump overboard and be drowned, or remain on the vessel and be burned. What a dreadful choice! Of course there was great confusion and distress on board that burning ship. Some were so terrified that they could neither move nor speak. Some cried; some screamed; some ran wildly about, wringing their hands, not knowing what they did. What could rubies or jewels do to comfort persons in such trying circumstances? Nothing whatever. Why, gold and silver and precious things lay scattered on the deck, and nobody would stoop to pick them up. But, in the midst of this scene of terror, over in one corner of the deck, as far away as possible from the fire, a little company of Christians were gathered together. They had then no thought of being saved, though two or three of them were saved, who afterwards told what I am now describing. In an hour or two they expected to be in eternity. And what are they doing? They are calm and cheerful. They have a Bible among them. A few verses are read.

RELIGION AND RUBIES COMPARED. 33

Then one of them prays. Then they talk about Jesus and that glorious heaven where they expect soon to meet. Then they read and pray again. They found comfort in their religion *then*, when nothing else in all the world could have given them comfort.

Religion is 'more precious than rubies' in the *way of comfort.*

But, fourthly, religion is ' *more precious than rubies* ' *in the* WAY OF ORNAMENT.

Rubies are chiefly used for ornament. We see them in breastpins or rings, on bracelets and head-dresses, and such like articles.

Rubies only adorn our bodies, but religion adorns our souls. We cannot eat rubies, or drink them. We cannot put them into our hearts, our eyes, our cheeks, our lips. They belong to the *outside* of us. But it is different with religion. This belongs particularly to the heart. It has its seat or dwelling-place in the heart; and from the heart it makes itself felt over the whole person. You know how much more beautiful a landscape appears if you look at it when the sun is shining, from what it is at night, or on a dark and cloudy day. But religion is the sunshine of the soul. It makes everything about it look bright and beautiful. We sometimes hear of people using different things to improve their complexion and make them look pretty. The things used for this purpose are called cosmetics. The meaning of cosmetic is, to make beautiful. But true religion is the best cosmetic in the world. It improves the looks of people more than anything else can. I have known people whose faces were naturally really ugly, but who were yet made so beautiful by religion that you could not look at them without admiring them. You know when Moses came down from talking with God on the Mount, his face was so bright and shining that it fairly dazzled people's eyes, like looking at the sun, and he had to put a veil over it before his friends could talk with him. It was his religion which did that. And so you remember the first martyr, St. Stephen, while preaching to the Jews, said: 'Behold I see the heavens opened, and the Son of Man standing at the right hand of God. And all that sat in the council, looking at him, saw his face as it had been the face of an angel.' It was the religion of Stephen which made his face look so beautiful. Religion has a wonderful power in adorning people, or improving their appearance. It gives them 'a meek and quiet spirit;' and this the Bible calls an 'ornament which is in the sight of God of great price.' Religion makes the eye look brighter, and the complexion clearer, and the smile sweeter, and the voice softer, and everything about our person better looking than it otherwise would be. You remember that we kept the last Washington's birthday as a sort of holiday. In the evening many of the finest houses in the city were illuminated. The blinds were up, and the gas or candles were burning, and the parlours were lighted up, so that as you went by you could see the beautiful paintings and statuary that were in them. What a wonderful change that illumination made in the appearance of those houses! But religion is the illumination of the soul. It lights it up in such a way as to show us beauties that we never should have seen without it. And yet it only just begins to do this in the present life. We never shall know till we get to heaven what ornaments religion will put upon us, or how beautiful it will make us appear.

You remember reading about the transfiguration of Jesus on the Mount. The disciples who were with Him saw His face shining with a brightness more dazzling than that of the sun. His garments became whiter than snow, and glittered and sparkled most gloriously. I suppose *that* was the most glorious sight ever seen in this world. And one of the reasons why Jesus was transfigured in that way was to give us, as it were, *a peep into heaven,*—to let us have just a glance at His glory. Jesus appeared on the Mount of Transfiguration just as He appears now in heaven. And He appeared in this manner in order to show us a pattern of the beauty and glory which He intends to put on all His people. If we love Jesus He will make us look at last, and look for ever, just as He looked Himself when He was transfigured. The Bible tells us that 'He will change our vile bodies, and make them like His own glorious body.' It tells us, too, that when 'He shall appear' again in the glory of His heavenly kingdom 'we shall be like Him.' What a sight it will be, when all who have loved and served Jesus shall be shining forth in beauty and glory just as He shone on the Mount of Transfiguration! The finest rubies in the world will only be like dark spots upon the sun compared to them. When you see an ugly-looking worm crawling on the earth, you can hardly think that some day it will put on beautiful wings, and go flying about in the sunbeams, all glittering with glory. But it will. And just such a change awaits the Christian.

A poor but very pious and Christian woman once called to see two rich young ladies. They were elegantly dressed, but they were Christians too, and without regard to her poverty and mean appearance they received her with great kindness, and inviting her into a splendid dining-room, sat down to converse with her upon religious subjects. While they were thus engaged, a brother of the young ladies happened to enter. He was a gay, thoughtless, proud young man. He looked greatly astonished to see his sisters engaged in conversation with such a poor, shabby-looking woman. One of them rose up directly and said, 'Brother, don't be surprised; this is a king's daughter, only she has not yet got her fine clothing on.'

In *the way of ornament* religion is more precious than rubies.

I will speak of one more point, and this is, that religion is 'more precious than rubies' in the WAY OF RICHES.

Rubies are very valuable. I saw a small one in a jeweller's shop the other day which they to'd me was worth about £40. Sometimes a ruby has been found that was worth several hundreds of pounds. But suppose that all the rubies in the world could be gathered together in one great, glittering pile. What a dazzling sight they would present! I cannot venture to guess how much they would be worth. But *this* I know very well, that whatever amount of money they might be valued at, though it were multiplied *ten thousand* times, it would still be true that religion would be more precious than rubies. In the *way of riches* it would be worth more than all those rubies put together. We consider a man rich if he is worth a hundred thousand pounds. But do you know how rich religion makes a man? Did you ever try to calculate how much a Christian is worth? Perhaps you would like to reckon it up. You can work it out by addition and multiplication. Let me tell you how to begin. The Bible tells us that Christians are 'joint-heirs with Christ.'—Rom. viii. 17. Now, you know that the heir of a man is the person who is to possess his property. '*Joint*-heirs' are those who share or possess property together. When we are told that Christians are 'joint-heirs with Christ,' it means that Jesus will share with His people all that belongs to Him. And how much is Jesus worth? He said Himself, '*All things* that the Father hath are mine.' Well, then, if you want to work out the sum that I was just speaking of, you must add up the value of all the gold, and the silver, and the gems, and the jewels, and the iron and brass, and the houses, and the lands in the world. And when you have written down the sum of all these, you must multiply it by the number of all the other worlds that God has made. That will tell you how much Jesus is worth, and when you find that out you will find how rich religion makes a Christian.

'See!' said a rich landowner to a poor peasant, as he pointed out to him the beautiful things around, 'those broad fields are mine. Those magnificent parks, those beautiful forests, those snug, smiling farms, and, in short, all you see on every side belongs to me.'

The poor peasant was a Christian. He had not much of worldly goods, but he felt that he was rich in faith, and an heir of God's glorious kingdom. He looked thoughtfully at the great landholder for a moment, and then, with the hope and joy of a Christian kindling in his eye, he pointed towards heaven, saying,

'And is *that* yours also?'

The lord of all those possessions was silent. He felt in a moment that *he* with all his property was poor, for he had nothing to take with him beyond the grave, while the humble peasant was really rich, for he was the owner of 'an inheritance incorruptible, and undefiled, and that fadeth not away.' In *the way of riches* religion is 'more precious than rubies.'

Now we have compared religion and rubies together in *five* different ways, and have seen that in each of them 'she is more precious than rubies.' In the *way of instruction* this is true; and so it is *in the way of help—in the way of comfort—in the way of ornament—and in the way of riches.*

And if this is so, then how earnestly we should seek this great blessing. Religion is the principal thing. It is 'the one thing needful' of which Jesus spoke when He was on earth. This was what He meant when He said: 'Seek *first* the kingdom of God and His righteousness.'

> ' Religion is the chief concern
>   Of mortals here below;
> May we its great importance learn,
>   Its sovereign virtue know.
>
> ' Religion should our thoughts engage
>   Amidst our youthful bloom;
> 'Twill fit us for declining age,
>   Or for an early tomb.
>
> ' Oh! may our hearts, by grace renewed,
>   Be our Redeemer's throne;

'And be our stubborn will subdued,
  His government to own.

'Let deep repentance, faith and love,
  Be joined with godly fear,
And all our conversation prove
  Our hearts to be sincere.'

III.

Lessons from the Ant.

'*Go to the ant,—consider her ways, and be wise.*'—PROV. vi. 6.

WHAT a very little thing an ant is! Some of them are so small that we can hardly see them. The largest of them are not longer than the end of your little finger. We might crush hundreds of them at a time by a single stamp of our foot. Many persons despise them. Very few think of them as they ought. But here Solomon, who was the wisest man who ever lived, sets up a little ant before us as our teacher. He says: 'Go to the ant,—consider her ways, and be wise.'

Suppose you should come to your class in Sunday school some Sunday morning, and find your teacher's chair empty. You would perhaps say to yourself, 'Well, we're not going to have any teacher to-day.' And suppose that while you were waiting, you should see a little tiny ant climb up into the chair. There you see it creeping up and up, and presently it gets on to the seat of the chair. You watch it narrowly to see what it is going to do. Pretty soon it takes its place right in the middle of the chair. There it lifts itself up on its hind legs in a kind of sitting posture. It puts on a grave, wise, knowing look. It makes a graceful bow of its little head, and begins to speak. How funny it would be! You look and listen very attentively. It says: 'My dear young friends, will you allow me to take your kind teacher's place to-day? I am a little mite of a creature, I know, but please don't despise me on that account. I don't know how to read, and I can't pretend to explain the wonderful things in the Bible that your teacher is accustomed to talk to you about. But I should like to tell you about myself, and the tribe of people that I belong to. We ants are a curious set of creatures. And yet I think you will be interested in some of our habits and customs, and perhaps you may learn some useful lessons from hearing about our ways of living.'

Now, if anything of this kind could take place, and your tiny little teacher could speak to you, she would have a great many interesting things to tell. She could tell you about the houses they live in, some of which are *forty stories high*,—twenty stories being dug out, one beneath another, under the earth, and twenty stories being built up over them, *above* ground: she could tell you about the different kinds of trades they follow,— how some are miners, and dig down into the ground; some are masons, and build very curious houses, with long walls, supported by pillars and covered over with arched ceilings. She could tell you how some are carpenters, who build houses out of wood, having many chambers which communicate with each other by entries and galleries; how some are nurses, and spend their whole time taking care of the young ones; some are labourers, and are made, like the negro slaves in the South, to work for their masters; while some are soldiers, whose only business it is to mount guard, and stand ready to defend their *friends and fellow-citizens*, in case of any attack being made upon them. These, and a great many other curious things, she could speak about. I am sure you would remember the lessons of your little teacher on that day as long as you live. But of course nothing like this will ever take place. We have only been *supposing* that it might—though we know very well that it can't. We know that ants can't speak, at least they can't speak *English,* and so can't make themselves understood by us, though there is no doubt that they have some way of speaking or of making themselves understood by one another. But though they are not able to come and teach us, yet *we can go to them and learn.* And this is just what Solomon tells us to do in the text. He says, '*Go to the ant,—consider her ways, and be wise.*' This is what we are now going to do. We are going to the ant 'to consider her ways,' that is, to inquire how she lives and labours, and to find out what useful lessons we can learn from her.

I wish to speak of *five* lessons we may learn from the ant.

The first of these is a lesson of INDUSTRY.

We speak of 'the little busy bee' as teaching us a lesson of industry, and so it does; but the ant is a better example of industry even than the bee. Suppose we go and look at one of these ant settlements. We may call it a village, or town of ants. It is underground of course. But suppose we could just lift off the covering, and look at what is going on, what a busy scene we should behold! This little town has more inhabitants than many large cities. Now let us go into the nursery department first. Here we look into a little room. The floor is covered all over with little white things, about the size of a grain of rice or wheat. These are called *larvæ.* They are the baby-ants. *Now* they don't look like ants at all, but rather like little grubs or worms. But they are the young ants, or ants in their baby-state. There are thousands upon thousands of them. And there is an amazing amount of work to be done for them. Those ants that you see there, going about among these babies, are the nurses. They have a pretty busy time of it, and need to be very industrious. Only see what they have to do. The babies must be kept clean. Hence you will see some of the nurses going about among the little ones and wiping off every bit of dirt they see upon them. They have no towels or napkins to do this with, but they do it very nicely with their hands, or what are called their *antennæ*, or feelers. Then these babies have to be fed two or three times a day, and to do this for so many of them is no small job. And then the babies require to be often moved about from one part of the house to the other. They must be kept in just a certain degree of warmth, or else they will die. The ants have no thermometers to tell how warm it is, for God has taught them to find this out without a thermometer. They can't regulate the heat in their nurseries as we can. When ours are too cool, we have only to stir up the fire and put a little more coal on. If it is too warm, we shut up the register from the grate, or open the room door, and the trouble is soon remedied. But when it is too cold in the ants' nursery they have to carry their babies to another part where it is warmer. Every morning, after the sun is up, they have to carry all their babies, one by one, to the upper rooms where the sunbeams make it warm. And then, before the sun sets, they carry them all down again to the lower rooms, where they are protected from the cold night air. And this they continue to do, day after day, as long as they live, without ever getting tired. What examples of industry these ants are!

And now let us go out of the nursery, and look at the working ants, or labourers. Here we may learn the same lesson of industry. These labouring ants have to pro vide food for their large household. All the day long they may be found toiling patiently, endeavouring to carry provisions to their homes. There is no better school in the world in which to learn the lesson of industry than in a settlement of ants. There are no idlers about their establishments. Every one has something to do. You will see one loaded with a grain of wheat, another with a dead fly, another with a bit of sugar, and another, perhaps, with a little piece of wood, which is wanted at home for some purpose or other. If an ant finds the body of some dead insect, such as a bee, for instance, which is too large for him to carry by himself, he will hurry back to the settlement, and get two or three of his friends to come and help him. Then they will take hold of it together, and never leave it till they get it home. If they find it too large to be carried into their door, they will break it up, and carry it in piece by piece. A gentleman saw an ant dragging along a piece of wood, so large that he could barely get on with it on level ground. By and by he came to a steep little hill in his way home. He tried to get up the hill, but the little log rolled him down again. He tried it four or five times, with no better success. Presently two other ants came along. The little fellow ran up to them, as if to tell them of his trouble. Then they turned back and helped him up the hill. As soon as they got on level ground again the two helpers went about their business, and left their friend to get on by himself.

They never leave home without having some special business to attend to, and never go back again without carrying something with them, or having news to tell of something useful which has been discovered, and which requires the help of others. And when one of them comes to tell that he has found a piece of sugar, or bread, or any kind of fruit, even though it is in the highest story of a large house, they immediately form themselves into a line, and march after their leader, till they reach the prize he has told them of, and then they work on, without stopping, till it is all stowed away in their homes. They work from morning till night, and when it is moonlight, at least, they often work all through the night.

What an example to lazy, idling people, whether young or old, the ants are, in this respect! Let us never despise these worthy little creatures. But when we feel tempted to indolence in our studies, or our work, let us think of the text, 'Go to the ant,—consider her ways, and be wise.'

Our first lesson from the ant is a *lesson of industry*.

Our second lesson from the ant is a lesson of PERSE-VERANCE.

The ant is quite as remarkable for its perseverance as for its industry. They never seem to get discouraged by the difficulties that meet them in what they are doing. If an unlucky horse or cow happens to tread upon their town, and crush a dozen or more of their houses, they stop whatever else they are doing, and go to work to repair the damage done. If the same thing occurs again the next day, or every day for a week, still they are ready, in a moment, to clear away the ruins and make the best of what they can't help.

A gentleman was once watching an ant-hill that had been broken up. He saw one of the nurses which had one of her hind legs taken off in the crash; yet she went to work at once to help to remove their young to a place of safety, and this poor wounded creature actually succeeded herself in carrying away *ten* of the baby ants to their new settlement before the repairs were completed. What wonderful perseverance that was!

Sometimes the ants have taught this lesson in a way that has led to very important results, when they little thought how much good they were doing. There was once a celebrated king and conqueror known as Timour the Tartar. On one occasion he was defeated in battle, and in fleeing from his enemies he sought shelter in an old ruined building. Here he was obliged to spend many hours, being afraid to venture out lest he should be seen, and taken or killed. Separated from his friends, alone, helpless, and not knowing what would happen to him next, he naturally felt very sad and discouraged. As he lay stretched out to rest himself upon the floor of the ruined building, thinking about what he should do, he noticed a little ant carrying something about as big as itself. He watched it as it made its way across the floor. Presently it came to the wall, and tried to get up with its load. But the burden was too heavy for it, and down they both tumbled together. Not discouraged, however, it tried again, and tumbled again. Again it tried, and again it tumbled. Still the persevering little creature wouldn't give it up. Timour became very much interested in watching the ant. Sixty-nine times she tried to get up the wall, and sixty-nine times she tumbled down. But she tried the seventieth time and succeeded. She carried her burden at last to the top of the wall.

Timour said afterwards to his friends, 'That sight gave me courage, and I never forgot it.' He went to the ant, considered her ways, and was wise. He learned a lesson of *perseverance*. This is one of the most important lessons we have to learn. All the good men, and all the great men in the world have learned this lesson. And if we want to be good and great we must learn it. We can't begin too soon. The very youngest of you, my dear children, even these little infant children, should learn and practise this lesson every day. Never say, 'I can't.' By God's help and by *trying* you can do almost anything.

I never quoted Latin in a children's sermon before, but I'm going to do it now. There is an old proverb, of just three words, which comes in so nicely here that I must quote it. The proverb is, 'Perseverantia vincit omnia.' The meaning is, *Perseverance conquers all things.* This is worth remembering. I suppose the ants don't understand Latin; but it is very clear that they understand all about this proverb, and they practise it well.

A lady once was going by a ropewalk. At one end of the building she saw a little boy, about nine years old, turning a large wheel. He had to turn that wheel five hours every day. He only received about ninepence a day for his work. But he had a poor sick mother at home, and he was glad to be able to do anything to help her.

'My little fellow,' said the lady to him, 'don't you ever get tired of turning this great wheel?'

'Yes, ma'am, sometimes,' said he.

'And what do you do then?' asked the lady.

'*I take the other hand.*'

That was right. It was a noble reply. That little fellow understood about the Latin proverb. He was practising upon it. I have no doubt that boy will make his mark in the world. It is a great thing to know how to *take the other hand.* Oh, don't give up, and begin to fret and cry, as soon as you feel tired, but just *take the other hand.* '*Perseverance conquers all things.*' The second lesson we learn from the ants is *a lesson of perseverance.*

But we go to the ant again for our third lesson, and this is a LESSON OF UNION.

I mean by this, that we may learn from them the benefits of being united, and of working together. Take a single ant, and what an insignificant little creature it is. You can blow it away with a breath. You can crush it with your little finger. If the ants should break up their union with one another, and try to live by themselves, or in little companies of half a dozen or a dozen together, very soon they would all perish. It is being united together that makes them strong, and enables them to build their houses, and store them with provisions, and take care of their young, and protect themselves from danger. The ants know this very well, and therefore they all go in strongly for union.

It is by their union with one another that the ants are often enabled to preserve themselves from being entirely destroyed. In some parts of South America the rivers overflow their banks, and flood the country around, at certain seasons of the year. In those places the ants build their houses from three to six feet high above ground. They do this, like the builders of the Tower of Babel, to protect themselves from being swept away by the floods. But even this does not always succeed. Sometimes the very tops of their highest houses will be overflowed. Then the ants have nothing but their strong union feeling to preserve themselves from destruction. They do it in this way. A number of the very strongest among them will go and take firm hold of some tree or shrub with their fore claws or feet. Then some others will take hold of their hind feet, and others again of theirs, till thousands upon thousands of them are bound together, forming a great living chain of ants, and thus they float upon the surface of the water, anchored safely to the tree by the strong grasp of their friends, till the floods have rolled away, and they can go back to their homes. Here we see how the ants are saved from destruction by their love of union.

And this union of the ants not only saves them from destruction, it *also enables them to do great good*, which they never could do if they were not thus united. In some parts of South America the ants act as the scavengers or sweepers, or cleaners of the country. They make their appearance in immense numbers, every two or three years, and their object seems to be to cleanse or purify the country. The people are glad to see them come, and throw open their houses for them to come in. The ants march in troops, like huge armies. They go through every room, find their way into every nook and corner, every hole and crack, and destroy all the rats and mice, and scorpions, and cockroaches, and other vermin, and then quietly go back to the forests where they came from.

An English gentleman was living in this part of the country once, who didn't understand the nature of these visits. He had not 'been to the ants to consider their ways.' He was not wise in regard to them. He was walking in his garden one morning, when he heard his servant calling out, 'The ants are coming! the ants are coming!' 'Well,' says he, 'let them come.' He didn't know what this meant. But on entering his house he found a solid column of ants, about ten inches wide, pouring like a stream of dark water into his dwelling. He seized a broom and tried to sweep them away, but in vain. He got some molasses and tried to stop their progress by pouring this out before them. But they passed on, making a bridge over the molasses, out of the bodies of their companions, and still they pressed on Then he got a kettle of boiling water, and poured it on them. But though he broke their ranks for a few moments, and destroyed vast multitudes of them, still, for every one killed there seemed to come a thousand more. Presently their broken ranks were formed again, and on they went. The Englishman was fairly beaten. He was obliged to surrender and leave his house in possession of these invaders. Soon after he had to go off on some business till the latter part of the day.

On speaking to one of the natives about what had occurred, the native told him that they considered these ants one of the greatest blessings. The Englishman shook his head, and said:

'Well, it seems to me you must be very badly off in this country for blessings, if you have to reckon these things among them.'

But when he came home in the evening he changed his mind. The house he occupied had been overrun with all sorts of vermin. On entering it there was not an ant to be seen. The only trace of their having been there was found in the scattered bones of rats and mice; the hard shells of beetles and roaches, their legs and wings, and the husks of eggs,—all of which had been devoured. The ants were all gone, and the house was left perfectly free from vermin. This *was* a blessing indeed. Those little creatures had come as missionaries of purity and cleanliness. And they had fulfilled their mission well. But if they had not been *united* together what could they have done?

And so it is with us. Whether in the nation—in the Church—in the Sunday-school—or in the family, it is a great blessing to be united. We can keep off a great many evils from ourselves, and do good to others in many ways, if we are united, which we never can do when separated. Let us learn from the ant a lesson of union! And let us do all we can to promote union:—

union in our country;—union in our Church;—union in our school;—union in our families. There is strength in union; there is safety in union; there is blessing in union.

But we 'go to the ant' again, and the fourth lesson we learn from her is a LESSON OF KINDNESS.

Although they have so much to do, and work so hard, they seem to be a very happy set of little creatures. Sometimes they have a little holiday, or recess time together, and then they may be seen having nice fun with each other. Their favourite amusement at such times is in wrestling and racing matches. And those who have spent much time in watching them say it is very amusing to notice their different tricks and pranks. A gentleman says he observed one species of ants, who at such times are very fond of carrying one another on their backs, very much after the manner that boys call *pig-a-back*. The ant to be carried will throw his front legs round the neck of the one that carries him, and cling to the other part of the body with his hind legs, and so hold on while he gets his ride, after the style of the celebrated John Gilpin, of whom the poet Cowper wrote so humorously. When they get through their rides they let each other down very gently. Boys and girls might learn a lesson in gentleness from seeing the ants at play.

There seems to be nothing like selfishness among ants. If one of their number has a heavier burden to carry than he can get along with, another will come and help him. They act faithfully up to that good Bible rule which tells us to 'bear one another's burdens.' If one of them is in trouble or distress, it excites the sympathy of the others, and they do all they can to help and comfort him. A gentleman who was watching some ants one day, took a pair of scissors and cut off one of the *antennæ*, or feelers, of a little fellow. It seemed to give him a good deal of distress and pain. Presently, some of his companions came up to him, and evidently pitying his distress, seemed to be trying to comfort him, and they actually anointed the wounded limb with some transparent fluid from their mouths.

Sometimes, when one of their labourers is accidentally wounded at his work, he is taken to one of their rooms, which is used as a kind of a hospital, where he is taken care of till he gets well again. But if they find he can't be cured, and isn't likely to be useful any more, they take no more care of him, but throw his body out among the rubbish of their settlement.

When the young ones are being fed, the nurses always attend to the smallest of them first; and the older ones never touch the food, but keep quiet and still, until their littler brothers have been fed and are satisfied. Here they set a very good example, and one worthy of being followed by the young in all our families.

If one of their companions is threatened with an attack, the others will all join together for his defence.

They are all the time trying to promote each other's welfare. Those who go abroad bring food home for those who are building their houses or taking care of their young. And if one of them, in going about, happens to find a lot of nice provisions, he scampers back as fast as he can to tell his friends at home about it, and to show them the way to it.

A lady once had a pot of molasses, which she found infested by ants. She tried various ways to keep them from getting at it, but all in vain. At last she fastened a cord round the vessel which held it, and let it hang down from a hook in the ceiling. Now it happened that there was just one single ant left upon that vessel. The lady thought she had swept them all off before she hung it up. But this little fellow had escaped her notice. When he found himself alone with that ocean of sweetness, he ate as much as he wanted. Then he mounted the rope. He climbed up it to the ceiling. He crossed the ceiling, he marched down the wall, and made straight tracks for home. As soon as he arrived he told his friends he had found the molasses, and was ready to show them the way. Directly a great company of them were ready to follow him. They formed in a line of march. He headed the line, and led them down that cord into the 'happy valley' at the foot of it. At once they attacked the molasses. Each one took a load and started for home. Pretty soon there were two lines of ants to be seen along that cord: one was going up, full —the other was coming down, empty. They never stopped till they had left that vessel perfectly clean of molasses. And when the good lady came to take down her molasses,—behold, it *wasn't there.*

Of course, ants never heard the eighth commandment. They know nothing about stealing. It is perfectly right for them to lay their hands on everything they find that suits them. And these things that I have mentioned show that they are real noble little fellows. They are polite and kind, full of tenderness and sympathy. They are always ready to help and comfort one another. They have no selfishness, but are ready at once to share all the good things they get with others. These are excellent qualities. And if we imitate the ants in these things, we shall be kind to the poor and needy. And when we have learned to love Jesus, and find how happy it makes us to serve Him, we shall want to send the gospel to those who are without it. Like the little New Zealand girl in England, who, when she became a Christian, wanted to go back to her own country and tell her friends about Jesus, we shall be ready to say— 'Do you think we can keep the good news to ourselves?' We learn from the ants a *lesson of kindness.*

We 'go to the ant' once more, and the fifth and last lesson we learn from her is a LESSON OF PRUDENCE.

The word prudence is made up of two Latin words, the meaning of which is looking ahead, or seeing before. You know what a telescope is. It is an instrument to help us to see things that are far off in regard to distance. The word telescope means seeing at a distance, or seeing through a distance. Now, if we could have a similar instrument to enable us to see things that are far off in regard to *time*, that would be a great invention. We might call it a *chronoscope*. That would mean an instrument for looking through time. Then, at the beginning of the year, we could just take a peep through our chronoscope, and tell, in a minute, all that was going to happen during the year. We should know when it was going to rain, and when the weather would be fine. We should know who was going to be sick, and who to be well,—who was going to live, and who to die. But that would be knowing more than would be good for us. God might have given us such an instrument if He had thought best. But it wasn't best, and so He has not given it to us. To take the place of it, however, He has given us what we call *prudence*. This means the power to think about the future and make preparation for it. And this *prudence* the ants have in a remarkable degree. I don't mean to say that the ants think and reason as we do. But still they act as though they did. God teaches them what to do without thinking, just as He does the birds, and the bees, and the beavers. And this power in animals, which enables them to know how to work and get their living, we call *instinct*. Nobody knows what instinct is, only it is that which enables animals to do, without thinking or learning, what we do by learning and thinking.

Solomon says, in the verses just after our text, that the ant, 'having no guide, overseer, or ruler, yet provideth her meat in the summer, and gathereth her food in the harvest.' It used to be thought that the ants lived all through the winter on the food which they laid up in the summer. But in our climate, when the cold weather comes, the ants remain in a torpid condition as if asleep, and don't need anything to eat. But it was different in a warm country like that in which Solomon lived. There the winters are not so cold as to put the ants to sleep, or make them torpid. But then they have long rainy seasons, too, in which ants can't go out to gather food. During those seasons they live on the food which they have laid up during the summer-time and harvest. And thus it is they teach us a lesson of prudence.

There is a fable told of The Ant and the Grasshopper. A poor grasshopper, who had outlived the summer, and was ready to perish with cold and hunger, happened to come near to a settlement of ants, who were living happily in their well-stored home. He humbly begged them to spare him a morsel of food from their plentiful stores. One of the ants asked him what he had been doing all summer, and how it happened that he had not laid up a stock of food as they had done. 'Alas! gentlemen,' said the poor, starving grasshopper, 'I passed the time merrily and pleasantly in drinking, singing, and dancing, and never once thought of winter.'

'If that be the case,' said the ant, 'all I have to say is, that they who drink, sing, and dance in summer, must *starve* in winter.'

We should follow the example of the ants while we are young, by preparing for the future of the present life. It is our summer, our harvest-time, while we are young. This is the time for us to get ready for what is before us when we become men and women. We should be diligent in learning all we can, and storing our minds with useful knowledge. This will help to make us useful and happy when we grow up. But if, like the grasshopper in summer, we are idle, and careless, and think of nothing but fun and frolic, we shall be ignorant and good for nothing when we grow up. Oh, then, my dear children, learn well from the ant this *lesson of prudence*. Form good habits now. Be industrious. Be persevering. Learn all you can now, and then, when you go out into the world, you will be ready to do your duty well. You will be loved and honoured by all who know you.

But we should follow the example of the ants also in preparing for the life to come. That life will never end.

This life is the harvest-time which God has given us, in which to make preparation for that life. I spoke a little while ago about a chronoscope, an instrument for looking into the future with, and finding out what we should do to make us ready for it. We have such an instrument. The Bible is our chronoscope for eternity. We can look through this, and see just what we want to make us happy after death. It shows us that we must have our sins pardoned, and our hearts changed:—we must love and serve Jesus. Then all that we do for Him will be like food prepared, or money laid up, for us in heaven. Eternity is like a long winter. Those who do not love and serve Jesus are going on to meet it without any preparation.

There was once a rich nobleman who kept a fool. This was a person whose office it was to do and say funny things, so as to make those about him laugh and be merry. The nobleman gave the fool a staff as a sign of his office, telling him to keep it till he found some one who was a greater fool than himself. Not many years after the nobleman was taken sick, and was going to die. The fool went to see him.

'I must shortly leave you,' said the nobleman.

'And whither art thou going?'

'Into the other world,' said his lordship.

'And when will you return again? within a month?'

'No.'

'Within a year?'

'No.'

'When, then?'

'Never.'

'Never?' said the fool; 'and what preparation and provision hast thou made for so long a journey, and for being happy there?'

'None at all,' said the nobleman.

'Here, then, take my staff,' said the fool, 'for with all my nonsense I am not guilty of such folly as this.'

LESSONS FROM THE ANT.

To be going into eternity without preparation is the greatest of all folly.

We have learned five lessons from the ant. These are, a *lesson of industry;* a *lesson of perseverance;* a *lesson of union;* a *lesson of kindness;* and a *lesson of prudence.* Now let us all pray God to give us grace to go and practise these lessons.

We are taught to pray—'that we may both perceive and know what things we ought to do, and also may have grace and power faithfully to fulfil the same.' Let this be our prayer, and then we shall be able with good effect to 'go to the ant,—to consider her ways, and be wise!'

IV.

The Hard Way.

'The way of transgressors is hard.'—Prov. xiii. 15.

HOW many different ways there are in the world for people to walk in! Some of these are rough ways, and others are smooth. Some are crooked ways, and others are straight. Some are broad, and others are narrow. Some are steep, and others are level. Some are pleasant, and others are unpleasant. Some are easy ways to walk in, while others are hard.

Our text tells us about *the hard way.* Solomon says, 'The way of transgressors is hard.' What does the word transgressor mean? It means, literally, *one who walks over.*

Suppose your school should go out into the country some fine summer day to have a picnic in the woods. It is a beautiful shady place to which you go, with a nice smooth velvet lawn spread out under the branches of the trees. But there is one part of the woods where the ground is low and marshy. At a little distance from this spot there have been some stakes driven into the ground, with a cord stretched along from one to another. When you all get out there, before you scatter to ramble through the woods and amuse yourselves, your superintendent speaks a few words to the scholars. He tells you that he hopes you will have a nice time, and enjoy yourselves very much. But there is one special thing he has to say. These are his words: 'You see those stakes, and the line stretched across them. No scholar here must cross that line. Under no circumstances whatever must any of you go over that line. This is the law for the day. You all hear it? You all understand it? You all promise to mind it? Then you are dismissed to play.'

Everything goes on pleasantly for a while. But by and by several of the boys are playing down by the stakes. Presently one of them sees a tree, with nice apples on it, a little distance beyond the forbidden line. 'Look at those ripe apples,' says he; 'come on, boys, let's go and get some.'

'No,' says one of the other boys, 'don't you see there's the line which the superintendent said we mustn't go over?'

'I should like to know what harm it's going to do, just to go over a few steps to get some nice apples. Besides, the superintendent won't know anything about it.' And so over he goes.

Now what is that boy when he goes over that line? He is a *transgressor*. He walks *over* the line which he was told not to walk over. So God's laws are the lines which He has set up to show us where we must not go; when we break those laws we *walk over* God's lines. That makes us sinners or transgressors; for the apostle says, 'Sin is the *transgression* of the law;' that means, it is walking over the line that God has set up for us. And in our text, Solomon says that 'The way of transgressors (or of those who walk over these lines) is hard.'

There are *three* things about the transgressor's way which make it hard. *The first of these is the* GUIDE *he has to follow.*

When we walk in the way of sin or transgression, our guide is Satan. You know the Bible tells us of all those who do not love and serve God, that Satan 'worketh' or ruleth in their hearts (Eph. ii. 2), and that they are 'taken captive by him at his will' (2 Tim. ii. 26). They are in his power. He is their guide or leader. So long as they are in the transgressor's way they can't get away from him, but are obliged to follow him as their guide; and to have such a guide must make that way a hard way. Let me try to show you how.

Suppose we were in Switzerland, and wanted to go to the top of Mount Blanc. That is a very dangerous mountain to go up. Nobody can get up without a guide. The way is very hard to find. In some places you have to walk over mountains of ice. At times the only path is just like a shelf of ice, not broader than your two hands, while at the side is a dreadful gulf, or chasm, hundreds of feet deep. Only think of a wall of ice higher than the top of a church steeple, and about a foot wide; and then think of walking along the top of that wall, with no railing on one side, and nothing to hold on to on the other. If you stumble or slip down you plunge, and are dashed to pieces. Why, it makes the head grow dizzy and the blood run cold just to think about it. This shows you why the travellers up that mountain need a guide. And it isn't *any* guide you would be willing to take. You want to be sure that your guide is *intelligent*, or that he knows the way well himself. You want to be sure that he is honest and faithful, so that he won't lead you into any unnecessary danger. And you want to be sure that he is strong and powerful, so that if you get faint on the way and need assistance he can help you. Sometimes in going over those dangerous passes, the guide ties a rope around the body of the traveller, and then fastens it to his own body, so that if the traveller should slip, he can stop him from falling; and many a one has been saved in this way.

And suppose now that in the valley of Chamouni, at the foot of Mount Blanc, from which travellers start to go up the mountain, there was a very wicked man acting as guide. He is so wicked that he undertakes to guide travellers up the mountain on purpose to destroy them. None who follow his guidance ever get safe down again. He either leads them to some slippery path, where they are sure to fall; or when they reach the middle of one of those high, narrow, icy paths, along the edge of a dreadful precipice, he gives them a push, and *down* they go to instant destruction.

Now, if you had to travel along such a mountain path, with such a guide to lead you, I want to know if you would not think *that* was a *hard* way to travel? Certainly you would. Well, Satan is just such a guide. His only object in guiding people is to lead them to destruction. Our journey through life is like a pathway over a dangerous mountain. We must have a guide. There are only two guides to choose between: Jesus is one, Satan is the other. If we take Jesus for our guide, He will lead us in Wisdom's ways; and 'her ways are ways of pleasantness, and all her paths are peace.' If we take Satan for our guide, he will lead us 'in the way of transgressors,' and we shall find that that is a *hard* way.

See, there is Judas Iscariot. He was one of the twelve apostles chosen by our Saviour to be with Him while He was on earth. But though he was *with* Jesus, he did not take Him for his guide. He allowed Satan to guide him. Judas was made treasurer of the company or society of the apostles. He kept the bag in which their money was put. Satan tempted him to steal some of that money. This was leading him into a slippery path. He didn't get as much money as he wanted. Then Satan put into his mind the horrible thought of betraying his Master, and selling Him to His enemies for thirty pieces of silver, or about three pounds, the price in those days of a common slave. Thus Satan led Judas to one of those narrow paths along the edge of an awful precipice. As soon as he had betrayed his Master, he tempted him to go and hang himself. When he did this, Satan pushed him off from that dangerous path, and plunged him into everlasting destruction. And this is what he tries to do to all transgressors who follow his guidance. 'The way of transgressors is hard.'

It is hard, in the first place, because of *the guide* which those who walk in it must follow.

But in the second place, ' *The way of transgressors is hard*' *because of the* RECOLLECTIONS *which those have of it who walk therein.*

Some years ago there was a good minister whose name was Dr. Doddridge. On one occasion he had a very singular dream. He thought in his dream that he was taken sick and died. His spirit left the body and soared away towards heaven under the guidance of an angel. After a long flight he arrived at the gate of the heavenly city. He entered. Then the angel introduced him into a very beautiful palace, where he was to remain. Here the angel left him, telling him he would find enough to interest him in those rooms till the Lord of the city came to him. Then he began to look round. The walls of the room were covered all over with paintings, which seemed to be wrought curiously into the materials of which the walls were made. On examining them closely, he was greatly surprised to find that these paintings formed a long series of pictures representing the history of his own life on earth. All that he had done—all that he had said, or thought, or felt—was here pictured out on the walls of the palace in which he was to live for ever. His sins which had been forgiven for Jesus' sake were not introduced; but every deed of kindness or charity—all that he had done to show his love for Jesus, or his desire to please Him—was pointed out there.

Now suppose we knew that God was engaged in taking photograph pictures of all our thoughts and feelings, our words and actions, during our whole lives. And suppose we knew that these pictures were to be fastened to the walls of the house in which our souls are to live for ever, so that they should be always before us, and that everybody might see them, then how very careful we should be to try and always have right thoughts and feelings, and always to speak and act in such a way that we should not feel ashamed to look ourselves, or to have any one else look, at the pictures of what we had been doing or saying or thinking or feeling. If we are trying to love and serve God, then all the pictures of our life, painted on the walls of our heavenly home, will be such as we shall love to look upon. This is one of the things which makes Wisdom's way a pleasant way. All the recollections we shall have of it hereafter will be pleasant recollections.

But it is very different with 'the way of the transgressor.' All the recollections of those who walk in this way will be painful. This is one of the things that make this way hard. I might tell you many stories to illustrate this part of our sermon, but I will only give you one. This, however, I hope you will never forget.

Henry Stanley was the son of pious parents. He was the eldest of a family of four boys, and was of a bold and daring disposition. One summer's morning, when he was twelve years old, his father came to him and said: 'Henry, my boy, this is your birthday, and I am going to give you and your brothers a holiday this afternoon; you may go into the fields, and take one or two of your companions with you.'

The afternoon came, bright and beautiful. Before starting, Mr. Stanley said: 'Henry, you are older than any of your brothers or friends; you must, therefore, set them a good example. Don't go through Farmer Clarke's field, for there is a dangerous bull there. Go round by the lane. *Now mind what I say.*' Mr. Stanley then told Henry to take great care of Frank, his youngest brother. Frank was a beautiful child, about six years of age, with bright dark eyes and rosy cheeks, the pride and pet of the family. At the close of the day the boys were to have tea with an old servant of their mother's named Burton, who lived in a neat pretty cottage at the foot of the lane. They set off in high glee, taking with them their dog 'Roughie.' Frank was very fond of Roughie, who was his constant companion. On this occasion Frank had tied a ribbon round his favourite's neck, so that they walked together the whole way. They expected to have a happy time, and so they would have had if Henry had only kept out of the 'way of transgressors.'

When they had gone some distance they came to Farmer Clarke's field and the lane, which were close together. Here they stopped. 'I wish we could only go through the field,' said Henry, in a fretful, grumbling tone; 'it's so much nearer. I'm sure the bull wouldn't hurt us. I don't think father knew we had Roughie with us, or I'm sure he wouldn't have forbidden us to go.'

'Oh, do come along the lane,' said his brother Alfred, 'it's not much farther; and if we go through the field we shall be disobeying father.'

'Well,' said Henry, 'let me stop and look through the gate; I should like at least to see this bull.'

Frank came to the gate with Roughie, and sat singing on the stile, tying flowers which he had gathered by the way on Roughie's neck. Presently he saw some bright ones growing on the bank, and knowing nothing about the bull, he slipped off the stile, ran into the field, and began to pick the flowers. Meanwhile, Henry looked through the gate, but saw nothing of the bull. 'It isn't here,' said he; but he had hardly spoken the words before he heard a low bellowing. Not in the least frightened, Henry climbed up the gate. At length he saw the bull approaching slowly, though he did not appear to see him. He then got down, not noticing Frank; he did not even look for him, as he thought he was with his brothers, who were walking up the lane. He next opened the gate, which was fastened very securely, saying, 'Now for some fun.' Thoughtless, wicked boy! Thus he went into the 'transgressor's way.' We shall see directly how *hard* he found it.

He picked up some stones, and, entering the field,

began to throw them at the bull. Directly the bull began pawing the ground and bellowing with rage. Now Henry was frightened, and ran out of the field, but *forgetting to fasten the gate after him*.

His brothers were gone some distance, and were seated on the bank at the roadside waiting for him. Henry came up panting for breath, and cried: 'You cowards! You were *afraid* of the bull! Why'—

Here Alfred interrupted him, saying in a quick, hurried tone, 'Where's Frankie? O Henry, why didn't you bring him with you?'

Henry stopped and turned pale. 'He must have come'— But here he was interrupted again by seeing the bull coming up the lane at full speed towards them. Henry shrieked with terror, and tried to follow his brothers, who were running with all their might. But presently the bull overtook him, tossed him high up in the air, and left him lying senseless in the road. In this state he was picked up and carried home.

And now you are all wondering what has become of dear little Frank. You remember he had slipped into the field to gather flowers. Roughie followed him. Presently the dog began to bark loudly, and ran away from Frank. This made Frank turn round, when he saw the bull running up to him. The poor child screamed, and called for his mother; but she could neither hear nor help him. The bull came on, and, running at Frank, tossed him over the hedge on to a hayrick which was in the next field.

Afterwards some men who were going by saw Roughie, who had climbed up on to the hayrick, where his little master lay bleeding, and was barking furiously. They lifted the dear boy down, and carried him to Mrs. Burton's cottage. They thought that he had only fainted, and tried everything to bring him to, but in vain. Then he was carried home and laid gently on the sofa. His poor mother—ah! think of her feelings!— was leaning over his pale, sweet face, when suddenly, *so* suddenly that she started back, his large dark eyes opened, and his gentle voice said, 'Dear, dear mother; kiss me, dear mother;' and then, before she could stoop down to kiss him, his eyes were closed, his lips were still, and a bright angel had received the spirit of dear little Frankie to carry it up to heaven.

It was a long time before Henry became conscious. When he first came to his senses, he found himself in a darkened room, with the curtains drawn closely round his bed. He raised himself on one side and listened; he heard some one sighing deeply. 'Mother,' he murmured softly. The curtains were opened. 'Mother, where is Frankie?—what has happened?'

'You have been ill, my child,' said his mother quietly; and smoothing his pillow, she laid his head down on it. Her face was calm and sorrowful, but there was no reproach in it. Henry seemed confused and bewildered. At length he said, 'Mother, have I been dreaming? What a fright I had! How strange it seems! But, mother, no! I've *not* been dreaming. I remember it all now. Oh! mother, tell me—*do* tell me where Frankie is!'

'In heaven, my child; dear little Frankie is a beautiful angel now.'

Ah! think how Henry must have felt then! He looked the very picture of heart-breaking sorrow. Seeing his great distress, his mother said—

'Frankie is happy now; we cannot wish him back again.'

'O mother, *I* have *killed* him! Can you ever forgive me? I never can be happy any more. My brother! oh, my brother!'

His mother let him cry in this way for a while, and then pitying the poor fellow's great distress, she said, 'Your father and I have forgiven you, my child, but now you must pray for the forgiveness of your heavenly Father.'

'Mother, won't you pray for me?' asked Henry.

His mother kneeled down at his bedside, and earnestly

prayed that God would forgive his great sin, and give him grace to keep out of the transgressor's ways for the future. This gave him a little relief; but, ah! no words can express the anguish of poor Henry's heart when he thought that his darling pet, his dear little Frankie, was in his tiny grave, brought there through *his* disobedience; and that he should never hear his merry laugh again when playing with old Roughie. Poor Henry! he had learned a *bitter* lesson indeed.

Slowly he recovered his health again, but he never, never forgot the scenes of that day. His whole life was embittered by the sad recollections of his twelfth birthday. And though he found peace at last through the blood of Jesus, and felt that God, for Christ's sake, had forgiven his sin, yet the *recollection* of it hung over him like a gloomy shadow. And suppose that we could have seen him months, or even years, after that melancholy event had taken place. He is going by Farmer Clarke's field. He stops at the gate. The whole scene comes fresh before him again. He bows down his head and weeps bitter tears. We go up to him and ask him to tell us what it is which makes 'the way of the transgressor hard.' He looks up, with his eyes full of tears, as he wrings his hands, and says, 'Oh, it's the *recollections!*— the *dreadful recollections!*'

The first thing that makes it hard is the *guide*. The second thing is the *recollections*. *The third thing I would speak of as making 'the way of transgressors' hard is the* WAGES.

Sometimes when a person is working for another, he is not paid all at once, but gets so much a week or month, and the rest when the work is finished. And this is the way in which God pays people for what they do in this life. So transgressors get part of their wages now, but the full payment will not be received till they get to the end of their hard way,—that is, till they come to die. Now the wages which transgressors receive are made up of two things, viz. *shame* and *suffering*.

E

Shame is a part of these wages. The Bible tells us that 'shame shall be the promotion of fools.' 'Fools' here means the same as 'transgressors.' And 'promotion' here means reward or wages. *Shame* is sure to be the wages of transgressors. This means that sin will always be followed by disgrace or shame.

Take some examples. The first transgressor that ever lived was Satan. He transgressed in heaven. He became proud. He was not willing to do and be what God wanted him to be and do. For this he was driven out of heaven. He was cast down to hell. And now, instead of loving and serving God, which is the highest honour,—yes, and the greatest happiness too,—he spends his whole time in doing what he knows God does not like: that is, in tempting men to commit all kinds of wickedness. Instead of being pure and holy, so that every one would love and reverence him, he is horribly vile and sinful. There is not a single person in all the universe that loves him. He is known as 'the old serpent,' 'a deceiver,' 'a liar,' 'a murderer,' 'the *evil one.*' Oh, what *shame* Satan has got from his transgression!

The next transgressors that we read of were Adam and Eve. They transgressed in the Garden of Eden. They ate of the tree of which God had forbidden them to eat. Then they felt that they were sinners. They knew that they were naked, and they were ashamed. When God came to speak to them they were afraid, and ran away, and tried to hide themselves among the trees of the garden. The mark of sin was on their souls. This made them feel ashamed to come before God.

The next transgressor was Cain. He transgressed by killing his brother. For this God put a *mark* upon him. Then he went forth a wanderer and a vagabond on the face of the earth. We do not know what the mark was which God put upon Cain, but it was something by which he might be known as a murderer, and yet which would keep others from murdering him. Suppose that God should cause a great blood-red spot, which could not be washed off or hidden from view, to come out on the forehead of every one guilty of murder, what a dreadful disgrace it would be to have such a mark! If the mark on Cain was something of this kind, then he must have been afraid to lift up his head in the presence of his fellow-creatures. No doubt he felt that shame, burning shame, was part of the wages of transgression. This helps to make this way hard.

And it is always so with those who walk in the way of transgressors. They may get money and find pleasure while walking in this way, but they are sure to cover themselves with disgrace. Let a person be known as a liar, a thief, a drunkard, and every honest, good man or woman will try to keep out of his way. We feel that it is a shame even to be known as the companions of such people.

There is the Apostle Paul. How everybody honours his name! What glory shines around it! Why is this? Because he kept out of the way of transgressors. He was faithful to his Master. But there is Judas Iscariot. He was an apostle too. But what different feelings are called up when his name is mentioned! It is black with disgrace and shame! Why is this? Because he went in the way of transgressors. He betrayed his Master. There is George Washington. Glorious name! What a halo of brightness and beauty shines round it! You feel your heart swell within you when you hear it. You are ready almost to take off your hat and make a low bow at the mere mention of it. All the world honours that name. They will do it while the world stands. Why? Because he was not a transgressor. He was a good man, and faithful to his country. But there is the name of Benedict Arnold. What feelings of unpleasantness and disgust are excited by this name! If you saw it on the ground you would be almost ready to trample it in the mire and dirt. It is a name covered all over with the foulest shame and dishonour. And why? Because he was a transgressor, a *traitor* against his country, the United States of America. He tried to sell his country for gold. He walked in the hard way, and he received part of his wages in *shame.*

Martin Luther used to say that if you wrestle with a sweep, whether you throw him down or he throws you, you are sure to be grimed and blackened with soot. Now sin or transgression is a sooty, blackening thing. Wherever it touches you it leaves a mark, and these marks are shameful.

Did you ever hear the story of Amos and the nails? There was a bad boy once whose name was Amos. His father was a very good man, and was grieved and troubled at the wickedness of his son. He had tried in vain to convince him of his sin, and induce him to do better. One day his father said to him, 'Amos, here is a hammer and a keg of nails. I wish you every time you do a wrong thing to drive one of these nails into the post.'

'Well, father, I will,' said Amos.

After a while Amos came to his father and said, 'I have used all the nails; the keg is empty. Come and see.'

His father went to the spot, and found the post black with nails. 'Amos,' said he, 'have you done something wrong for each of these nails?'

'Yes, father,' said the boy.

'O Amos,' said his father sorrowfully, 'how sad this is to think of! Why will you not turn about and try to be a good boy?'

Amos stood thoughtfully for a few moments, and then said, 'Father, I'll try. I know I have been very bad. Now I mean to pray God to help me to do better.'

'Very well,' said his father; 'now take the hammer, and every time you do a good act or resist a wrong one, draw out a nail and put it in the keg again.'

After some time the boy came to his father, and said, 'Come, father, and see the nails in the keg again. I have pulled out a nail for every good act, and now the keg is full again.'

'I am glad to see it, my son,' said his father; 'but see, *the marks of the nails remain.*'

So it is with transgression; it always leaves its marks. These marks it is a shame to bear. This shame is part of the wages which those must receive who walk in this hard way.

Another part of these wages is *suffering*. If you put your finger in the fire it will burn, and the burning will hurt you. God has made our bodies so that burning causes great suffering, in order to make us keep from going too near the fire. And He has made suffering part of the wages of transgression, in order to keep us from sin. If we should go out to the almshouse, and find out the history of those who are insane, or sick and suffering in other ways, how many sad illustrations we should find of the truth of our text, 'The way of transgressors is hard'! But I want to give you a very striking illustration of it that occurred once among some boys in a school.

Bob Winslow was the worst boy in the village. His father never checked him, but let him have his own way, till he had grown to be the terror of the neighbourhood. He particularly loved to make sport of old, lame, crippled persons. There was one poor woman bent down by age and infirmities that Bob used especially to make game of. She came every day, leaning on her crutch, to draw water from the well near her house, and just within the playground of the school-house. Bob would sometimes follow close behind her, pretending to be lame, and hobbling along on his umbrella for a crutch, and mimicking her motions. 'Only look at her,' he would say, 'isn't she like the letter S with an extra crook in it?' One day when he was doing this the old woman turned round, and looking at him reproachfully, said, 'Go home, child, and read the story of Elisha and the two bears out of the wood.'

'Shame on you, Bob!' said Charles Mansfield, one of the best boys in the school—'shame, I say, to laugh at the poor woman's misfortunes! I've heard my grandmother say that she became a cripple by lifting her poor afflicted son, and tending him night and day.'

'Shame! shame on you!' said Charles, and 'Shame, shame!' echoed from each of the boys present. '*You may get your own back broken* one of these days, Bob,—who knows?'

Charles Mansfield sprang to the old woman, and said, 'Let me help you to draw the water.' Then he kindly took her pail, filled it at the well, and carried it home for her, and the boys made an arrangement for one of them to come every day and fetch her a pail of water. 'God bless you! God bless you all! dear boys,' said the old woman, as she wiped away her tears, and entered her poor lonely home.

Bob Winslow's conduct was reported to the master. He was very much grieved, and sentenced him to stay in school and study, instead of going out to play at recess, for a week. This was pretty hard punishment, for Bob had very little love for study, but was very fond of play. Yet this was a slight punishment compared with what he was so soon to receive.

On the second day of his confinement, he sat near the open window, watching the boys at their sports in the playground. Suddenly, while the master was occupied in another part of the room, he rose and jumped from the window into the midst of the boys, with a shout at what he had done. 'Now let him punish me again if he can!' cried he. As he said this he ran backwards, throwing up his arms in defiance, and shouting, when—suddenly his voice ceased; there was a heavy plunge, and a loud groan burst on the ears of his startled companions.

It so happened that the well of which we have spoken was being repaired. The workmen were at a distance collecting their materials, and had carelessly left the opening of the well uncovered. As Bob was going backwards, at the very moment of his triumph he stepped into the mouth of the well, and down he went. There was a cry of horror from the boys. They all rushed to the spot. Charles Mansfield, the bravest of them all, was the first to seize the well-rope. He jumped into the bucket and got the boys to lower him down. The well was deep; but, fortunately, there was not much water in it, and Bob lay motionless at the bottom. Charles lifted him carefully, and with one arm round his apparently lifeless body, the other on the rope, he gave the signal, and was slowly raised to the top. The pale face of the wicked boy filled his companions with horror. Without saying a word they carried him to the house of the poor woman whom he had treated so cruelly. She had seen the accident from her window, and was hobbling along on her crutch to meet them. Poor Bob was taken into her humble home, and laid upon her bed. The kind-hearted old woman, forgetful of his ill-treatment of her, got out her bandages, her camphor bottle, and other things; and while one of the boys ran for the doctor, and another for their teacher, she sat down by his side, and bathed his hands and his forehead as tenderly as though he had been her own son. After the doctor had dressed his wounds he was carried on a litter to his own home, surrounded by his sorrowing companions, but still insensible.

A few hours later in the day a group of boys met on the playground. They talked to one another in a low voice. They looked pale and sad. Presently Charles Mansfield came up.

'Well, boys, how is poor Bob now? Have any of you heard?'

'O Charlie!' cried several at once, as they gathered round him, 'oh! don't you know? Haven't you heard? Why, he has opened his eyes and is able to speak; *but the doctor says he will be a cripple and a hunchback for life!*'

Charles clasped his hands without uttering a word, and burst into tears. He couldn't speak for a while. At last, with the tears still streaming down his pale cheeks, but with a manly voice, he said, 'Boys, I hope we shall never forget the lesson we have learned to-day. The Bible says, "The way of transgressors is hard;" and poor Bob's experience proves how true that is!'

I cannot tell you the dreadful suffering, both of mind and body, that Bob passed through during the months that he lay upon that sick bed. He found out that it is the *wages* of the transgressor which makes his way so hard. Great suffering indeed he passed through as part of the wages he had to receive.

I am glad to be able to tell you that Bob became a Christian on that bed of suffering. His sin was forgiven. Like Amos, he drew the nails out of the post; but ah! in his poor crippled back the *marks of the nails remained.* 'The way of transgressors is hard.' The *guide*, the *recollections*, and the *wages*, make it hard. The wages are made up of *shame* and *suffering*.

My dear children, we have all been in this way. Jesus came to show us how to get out of it. His blood takes away transgression.

If Jesus is our friend, we have nothing to fear. Martin Luther says, that Satan came to him one day and said, 'Luther, you are a great sinner, you will be lost.' 'Stop, stop,' said Luther, 'not so fast; one thing at a time, if you please. You say I am a great sinner. That is true, though you ought to be the last to say anything to any one about sin. I am a great sinner. Yes, but Jesus is a great Saviour. His blood cleanses from all sin; and, therefore, though I am a great sinner I shall go to heaven. I shall not be lost.' Then Satan went off and had nothing more to say. This is true. Jesus can pardon all our sins. If our sins are forgiven, for His sake, we never can be lost. Oh, turn to Jesus, then. Trust in Him. He will take you out of the hard way, and put you in that way which is all pleasantness and peace. As long as you live remember this text: 'The way of transgressors is hard!'

V.

The Sunday-school Garden.

'*I am come into my garden.*'—CANT. v. 1.

IT is Jesus who is speaking here. He says He is come into what? His garden. Yes. 'I am come into my garden.' By the *garden*, here, Jesus means His Church. He compares His Church unto a garden. But the Sunday-school is one of the most important parts of the Church of Christ. It is the nursery in which the young plants and trees are reared, which are afterwards to be set out on earth and in paradise above. We may consider the garden here, then, as referring to the Sunday-school. And then Jesus speaks about *coming into* this garden. Now, when we read or hear about this, I suppose we all feel inclined to ask two questions. These questions will form the divisions of our sermon. The questions are these: *Why is the Sunday-school like a garden? and what does Jesus come into it for?*

Why is the Sunday-school like a garden? It is so *because of what is done for it.* It is so *because of what grows in it.*

The Sunday-school is like a garden because of what is done for it. Now just see what we do for a garden when we wish to make one, and you will see that Jesus does the very same things for the Sunday-school.

The first thing done for a garden is to *fence it.* If you

want to make a garden out of a part of a field or common, you begin by building a fence all round it. This is to keep the cattle out, and to protect it from being trodden down by those who pass by. And so Jesus has fences all round the Sunday-school. These fences are made out of the commandments He has given us in the Bible. When we find a text in the Bible which tells us not to do anything, the words of that text are like a fence which God has set up to keep us from doing evil.

There was a little boy once who had been well taught in the Sunday-school. His mother was poor but pious. Her boy had learned to obey her. He had to go to sea as a cabin-boy. His mother's last words to him were—'*Johnny, never drink a drop of rum.*'

All the sailors used to drink liquor several times a day. They tried to persuade Johnny to drink, but he never would. One time, during a storm which lasted several days, they told him he would catch cold and die if he didn't take some liquor; but he wouldn't mind. At last, one of the sailors, who had never spoken to him on the subject, said he was sure he could make him take a drink. He went to try. He said everything he could think of to persuade him to drink. The little fellow heard all he had to say. Then he quoted his mother's words—'*Johnny, never drink a drop of rum.*' He repeated the fifth commandment, and a great many passages of Scripture about obedience to parents. The sailor hadn't heard so much of the Bible for a long time. He found he could not succeed, and gave it up. When he went back to his place, the other sailors asked him how he had made out. 'Oh,' says he, 'you can't do anything with him. Why, he's *brim full of the Bible.*'

You see, the Bible was a fence to keep Johnny from drinking. In the same way it has fences to keep us from all sinful things.

When we have fenced our garden, the next thing to do is *to* WEED IT. Weeds always grow thicker and faster than the plants and flowers in a garden. You can't do anything till the weeds are pulled up. But you may ask, what are the weeds that grow in God's garden? This garden, you remember, is made up of His children in the Sunday-school, and the weeds in it are the wrong feelings sometimes found in our hearts. *Pride* is one of these weeds. It is a tall, strong weed, with a glaring, disagreeable flower. It springs up and grows everywhere. It can grow where nothing else can; and it is very hard indeed to root out. *Anger* is another of these weeds; *impatience* is another; selfishness is another; idleness is another; disobedience is another; and so I might go on making out a long list. There is hardly any end to the weeds that grow in this garden, if they are only let alone. But all these must be pulled up. When we become the friends and followers of Jesus, He expects us to put away from us all these bad feelings and tempers. And when we do this we are pulling up weeds from His garden.

Now we've got our garden *fenced* and *weeded*. The next thing to be done for it is to *improve the soil*. Some soil is so very poor that nothing will grow in it. When this is the case, the gardener has many ways of curing it. I will only speak of one. He will have the poor soil taken away, and some good, rich soil put in its place. You know, if you go into the woods, where the leaves have been falling and mouldering away for a great many years, you have only to scrape away the dry leaves from the top, and underneath you find plenty of nice, soft, black, rich soil, which is the very thing to make first-rate garden-beds out of. Oh, how the plants and flowers will grow in this new soil! The gardener improves the soil by changing it and making it new.

And this is just what Jesus does to His people. He improves the soil of their hearts by changing it and making it new. He says in the Bible—'A new heart also will I give them, and a new spirit will I put within them; and I will take away the heart of stone from them, and will give them a heart of flesh.' This is like taking away the bad soil, in which nothing will grow, from a bed in the garden, and putting good, rich soil in its place. When Jesus makes our hearts new He is improving the soil of His garden. Everything that Jesus loves will grow in the soil of the new heart.

Well, here is the garden *fenced* and *weeded*, and with *its soil improved*. What next is to be done? Now we are ready to sow the seed, and put in the plants we want to have growing there. Here we want to have a bed of pinks and sweetwilliams, and so we put those seeds in. There we want a bed of marigolds and wall-flowers, and we sow the seeds for them. Over there we want to have some verbenas, and down this walk we want to have a large bed of mignonette, so as to perfume all the air. On the other side of the walk we want a tulip bed, so we set out the roots of this beautiful plant. Under our window we plant a sweet-brier and a honeysuckle, and in the bed opposite the window we set out a great variety of rose bushes. We can't expect to have a garden unless we put in the seeds and plants that we wish to have growing there.

But does Jesus do anything like this in His garden? *Certainly* He does. You know when Jesus was on earth, among the many beautiful parables which he spoke to the people was one about the sower. His disciples didn't understand it, and came and asked Him to explain it to them. In doing this, He told them that He Himself was the sower. He told them, also, that 'the seed was the word of God.' The truths of the Bible are this seed. It is called 'good seed.' When we read the Bible, and learn the truths it teaches, we are sowing this 'good seed' in our hearts, where it will grow like the different kinds of seed that we put in our gardens.

And then there is one other thing that must be done for our garden. It is fenced, and weeded, the soil is improved, and the seeds and plants are put into it.

Now it must be *watered* and *cared for*. Suppose no rain comes down and no dew distils upon it, will the seed sown there ever spring up and grow? Never. Or suppose the rain should fall, but no warm sun should shine upon it, will anything grow there? No. Sometimes the gardener lays pipes down in his garden, to carry water to different parts of it, so that when there comes a dry spell in summer he can easily water these plants and keep them from withering. And then, when the seeds spring up, and the plants begin to grow, how carefully the gardener watches them! How he loosens the soil, and picks out the stones, and tries to keep off everything that would hinder the plants from growing!

And just in this way Jesus waters and cares for His garden. His grace is the rain and dew that soften the soil of our hearts. His Holy Spirit is like the sun that shines on and warms them. Jesus has pipes in His garden to carry the water of His grace wherever it is needed. The Bible that we read and have explained to us is one of these pipes. The sermons that are preached to us, the prayers that we offer, and the sacraments ordained in the Church, are all precious, golden pipes, by means of which Jesus waters His garden. And then our blessed Saviour watches carefully over His garden all the time to keep anything from hurting the plants, or from hindering their growth.

Thus we see that the Sunday-school may be called a garden *because of what is done for it. It is fenced; it is weeded; the soil is improved; seeds and plants are put into it; and it is watered and cared for.*

But then there is another reason why the Sunday-school may be compared to a garden, viz. *because of what grows in it.*

In a garden we expect to find beautiful flowers and delicious fruit. Roses and lilies, and honeysuckles, and pinks, and daisies, and flowers of all kinds, are growing there. And fruits as well as flowers are found in our gardens. Apricots, and peaches, and pears, and grapes, and currants, and strawberries, and pleasant fruits, of oh how many kinds, grow and ripen there!

And so in the Sunday-school, which is the garden of Christ, many sweet flowers and fruits are found growing. Every good feeling that we cherish in our hearts is a spiritual flower, and every good deed that we perform in our lives is a spiritual fruit, which Jesus loves to see blooming and ripening in His garden. Let us look at some of these.

Here is a little girl who feels that she is a sinner. When she thinks of her sins, she feels very sorry. The thought of them makes her bosom swell. It brings the tears into her eyes. They flow down her cheeks. She bows her head and prays thus: 'Lord Jesus Christ, be merciful to me a sinner. Create in me a clean heart, and renew a right spirit within me.' This is repentance. Repentance is a spiritual flower. Jesus loves to see it. We may compare it to a snowdrop. This is a beautiful white flower which springs up before the snow is quite gone. It hangs down its delicate little head, just as if it had been doing something wrong, and was sorry for it. Every boy and girl who repents, *i.e.* who is truly sorry for sin, is a spiritual snowdrop in the garden of Jesus.

But see, here is a *crocus*. This is a sweet flower of a bright yellow colour. Like the snowdrop, it is one of the early spring flowers. It comes out while the ground is hard, and the air is cold, and the dry leaves scattered around make the garden look very dreary. And then its beautiful face looks so bright and sunshiny that we always think of this flower as representing *cheerfulness*.

'Poor Annie,' said a Sunday-school teacher one day to a little girl in her class who had no father, and whose mother was very poor and sick. 'Poor Annie!' 'Please, teacher, don't call me poor,' said the little girl; 'why, I've got a dear mother who loves me.' She loved Jesus, and was happy and cheerful. She was a smiling crocus in the garden of Jesus.

The father of a family had died very suddenly.

THE SUNDAY-SCHOOL GARDEN.

Shortly after, the minister called to sympathize with the widow and her fatherless children in their sorrow. As he entered the house, he met a bright-eyed little fellow about four years old. 'Well, Willie, you have no father now,' said the minister. 'No,' said Willie, 'I haven't any father,' and his large blue eyes filled with tears, 'but I've got a mother, though, and I've got a James, and a William, and a Lizzie, and a Hannah,' naming over all the members of the family that were left. Happy, cheerful spirit! there was another crocus in the garden of Jesus.

But see, here is a *honeysuckle*. It can't stand by itself. It must have something to cling to. But give it a cord, or pole, or branch to grow on, and it will twine itself around it, and cling fast to it, and grow finely, and fill all the air with its fragrance. Faith, or trust in God, is like the honeysuckle. It twines itself around God's promise, and clings to that, and then opens its beautiful fragrant flowers.

'What do you do without a mother to tell all your troubles to?' asked a little girl who had a mother, of one who had lost hers. 'Mother told me who to go to before she died,' said the orphan; 'I go to the Lord Jesus; He was mother's friend, and He's mine.'

'But Jesus is far off in the sky, and has a great many things to attend to; it's not likely He'll stop to mind you,' said the other.

'I don't know anything about that,' replied the orphan; 'all I know is, *He says He will, and that's enough for me.*' See how the trust of this dear child twined itself round God's promise, and grew there. *Trust*, or faith, is the *honeysuckle* in God's garden.

And then *contentment* is the *heart's-ease* here; and *humility* is the *violet;* and love is the myrtle; and modesty is the lily; and innocence is the daisy; and so we might go on all through the garden.

But there are *fruits* in God's garden as well as flowers. I said, you know, that good feelings in our hearts are the flowers that grow here. The fruits that ripen in God's garden are *good actions* in our lives. *Self-denial* is one of these fruits. *Charity*, or kindness to the poor and suffering, is another. *Forgiveness* to those who injure us is another. *Patience* is another, *perseverance* is another, *prayer* for God's blessing on ourselves and others is another, and so I might go on and mention a great many others. Now let me give you a sample or two of these fruits when they become ripe. Here is a sample of the fruit *forgiveness of injury.*

A slave in one of the West India Islands was noticed by his master very carefully watching over a poor broken-down negro who had been bought with a lot of others some days before. He shared his bed with him; fed him at his own table; carried him into the sunshine when cold, and into the shade when the sun was hot. He was so very kind to him that his master thought he must be a near relation, and he inquired if he were his father.

'No, massa,' was the answer.

'Is he an elder brother?'

'No, massa.'

'Perhaps he is your uncle, or some other relation?'

'No, massa, no relation; he not even my friend.'

'Then why are you so kind to him?'

'He my enemy, massa,' said the slave, 'he sold me to the slave-dealer; but my Bible tell me, when my enemy hunger, feed him; when he thirst, give him drink.' What a lovely fruit this was!

Here is an example of *submission to God*, which is another of the fruits that grow in this garden. A little girl had been attacked with sudden pain in the head, which ended in her becoming blind. She was taken to a celebrated eye-doctor, who examined her eyes, and then took her mother aside, and told her that nothing could be done for her daughter. The poor child wanted to know what the doctor said about her eyes. Her mother told her. 'What, mother!' exclaimed the child; 'am I never more to see the sun, nor the beautiful fields and flowers; nor you, my dear mother, nor my father?' She wrung her hands in sorrow and wept bitterly. Nothing seemed to give her the slightest comfort, till her mother took a pocket Bible from the table, and put it in her hands.

'What is this, mother?' inquired the poor, sorrowing child.

'It is the Bible, my dear,' said her mother. In a moment the poor sufferer became quiet. She thought at once of one after another of the sweet texts she had learned in that blessed book. She paused, turned her poor sightless eyeballs towards the ceiling, and a sweet, angel-like expression played over her face, while she breathed forth in earnest, though gently whispering tones, the words—'*Thy will be done on earth as it is in heaven.*' Ah! that was a precious fruit; and just what we might expect to find in God's garden.

It is surprising what a great amount of excellent fruit will often grow in this garden from the very smallest seed.

In London there is a large building called Exeter Hall. It is used chiefly to hold religious meetings and anniversaries in. Once they were holding a Sunday-school anniversary there. A clergyman was addressing the children. He told them about two bad little boys whom he had once known, and a good little girl whom he afterwards learned to know. One day this little girl was going home from Sunday-school, where she had learned to try to be like Jesus, 'who went about doing good.' On her way home she saw two little boys about her own age quarrelling. She went up to them, and told them how wickedly they were acting. She made them stop quarrelling, and finally persuaded them to go to her Sunday-school. The boys were named Jim and Tom. The girl was called little Mary Wood.

'Now, children,' said the gentleman, 'would you like to see Jim?'

With one voice they all shouted, 'Yes.'

'Jim, stand up,' said the gentleman, looking to another part of the platform. A tall, reverend-looking gentleman, dressed in black, and wearing a white cravat, arose and looked smilingly upon the children.

'There,' said the speaker, 'that is Jim. He has been a missionary for several years in one of the South Sea Islands. Now would you like to see Tom?'

'Yes, yes, sir,' was heard all over the house.

'Here he is,' said the speaker, straightening himself up; 'he, too, has been a missionary for years.'

'And now would you like to see little Mary Wood?'

'Yes, yes; oh, yes!' burst forth in a perfect storm of voices.

'Well, do you see that lady over there, with a black velvet bonnet, putting down her veil, and blushing like a rose? That's little Mary Wood. And now I have a secret to tell you. *She is my wife!*' That good girl sowed a very little seed in God's garden. The fruit which it bore was, two missionaries to the heathen, with all the good resulting from their labours.

But *prayer* is the plant in this garden on which the fruit grows most abundantly. Let me tell you about the fruit yielded by the prayer of a little child. Her name was Minnie. Her home used to be a very happy and comfortable one; but her father had taken to drinking. This had brought them to great poverty, and almost broken her poor mother's heart. One evening he came home just as Minnie had kneeled down to say her prayers. Hearing her little voice, he stood still a moment as he entered the room, and listened. The dear child was praying thus: 'O God! make father leave off his evil ways; make him my own dear father once again. Make dear mother's sad looks go away, and make her old smile come back; but Thy will be done!'

Minnie's mother burst into tears as she threw her arms around her husband's neck, and said, 'Oh, my husband, for the sake of that dear child, let us all be happy again!'

The poor man bowed his head and wept. Then, clasping his hands, he said, 'By the help of God, you shall have no more sorrow on my account.' And he kept his word. Dear little Minnie's prayer saved her father from going down to a drunkard's grave.

Wasn't that a precious fruit that grew on the plant of prayer? I might give you a great many more samples of the same kind. But there is no time. I must hasten on to the other part of our subject. Perhaps I have said enough to show why the Sunday-school is called a garden. It is called a garden *because of what is done for it, and because of what grows in it.*

But then there is another question we were to ask about this garden, and that is, *What does Jesus come into it for?*

He comes for *three* things. One of these is, to *watch the growth of the plants.* If you have a bed which you call your own in your father's garden, you feel a great interest in watching the flowers every day, and seeing how they grow. You will go into the garden every morning, and notice every new leaf that opens, and every fresh bud that appears. If you find the ground getting hard, you will loosen it. If it be dry, you will water it. If one of your plants seems weak and drooping, you will put a stick in for it to lean on. If it shoots out a long slender branch, you will be very careful to train it in the right direction, and to tie it up to the trellis, or to a stronger branch of the bush, so as to keep it from trailing on the ground. If you find a worm gnawing at the root, or insects eating away the leaves of your flowers, you will take them away, and do everything you can to make them grow and flourish. And this is just what Jesus does in His garden. Only He does a great deal more, and does it better too, than we can. You know we can't be all the time in our garden. We are obliged often to go away and leave it for hours, and perhaps for days together. Jesus never leaves His garden. He is in it all the time. He says in one place in the Bible, 'I will water it every moment; lest any hurt it, I will keep it night and day.'—Isa. xxvii. 3. Jesus is in His garden now. He is here this afternoon. He is in our school every Sunday, watching the plants and flowers whether they grow and flourish. He looks to see if we are minding our teachers, and listening attentively to learn the lessons taught us in His blessed Word. Suppose we could see the glorious Saviour walking up and down between the classes, and watching us, how should we feel? We can't see Him; but *He is here.* We can't see Him in our school—but He is there. He says in our text, 'I *am* come into my garden.' This doesn't mean that He comes once a year—but that He is doing it all the time. He is *always* in His garden. He is there, ready to hear us when we pray, ready to help us when we need, ready to guide and comfort and bless us. Oh, remember the text whenever you enter the school and take your seat in your class. Think that you hear Jesus say, 'I am come into my garden.' He comes to see what flowers are opening,— what fruits are ripening. He comes to *watch the growth of the plants.* This is one thing for which He comes.

Another thing for which He comes is, *to enjoy the beauty of the flowers.* If you have a garden, and are fond of flowers, you will find great enjoyment in it. You take pleasure in walking about to watch the seeds as they spring up, and see the new leaves and sprouts shoot forth from the plants. When your rose bush begins to bloom, what interest you take in noticing how the buds swell out more and more, till at last they burst open and unfold all their beautiful leaves to your sight! You love to smell the sweet fragrance of the flowers, and you love to watch the different appearance which they present from day to day. And now, perhaps, you are ready to ask, But can Jesus have any such feelings as these in reference to His garden? Certainly He has.

No gardener ever took half as much delight in the flowers he is raising as Jesus takes in His. Every Christian child, and every one who is trying to become a Christian, is a flower in the Saviour's garden, and nobody can tell how much pleasure Jesus takes in watching them. No mother ever loved her darling child as Jesus loves His children. It says in two places in this book of Canticles, where our text is, that ' He feedeth among the lilies.'—Cant. ii. 16, vi. 3. This shows us what delight He takes in being among them. You know there are two things about a flower which are pleasing: these are its sweet smell, and its beautiful colour. It is very pleasing to know that Jesus calls children who love and serve Him, His flowers. Yes; when we are trying to overcome all proud, or angry, or selfish feelings, and to be kind, and gentle, loving, and obedient children, then we are flowers in the garden of Jesus, more pleasing to Him than the most fragrant bud is to us when it blooms in its beauty and fills the air all round with its fragrance.

We love to do anything that we know will give pleasure to our parents and friends; how much more should we love to do what we know will be most pleasing to our glorious Saviour! He loves above all things to see the plants in His garden growing and bearing flowers. He *enjoys the beauty of the flowers.* This is what He comes into His garden for. Oh, who would not wish to be one of the flowers of Jesus?

But then there is another thing for which He comes into His garden. *He comes to gather the flowers.* When a gardener is walking through his garden, if he sees a flower more beautiful than the rest, and which pleases him very much, he will be very likely to pluck that flower from the stem on which it is growing, and put it in his bosom, where he can admire its beauty and enjoy its fragrance; or perhaps, if he has a conservatory or greenhouse opening into his parlour or study, he will take up the plant which bears that sweet flower, and put it in a flower-pot, and have it placed among the very choicest flowers in his greenhouse, where it will be sheltered from the frost and the cold air, and will have better care taken of it than it can have while growing out in the garden.

And does Jesus do anything like this in His garden? Certainly He does. You know how many dear children die while they are quite young. Well, what becomes of them? Ah! they are the flowers which Jesus has gathered and placed in His own bosom, or which He has transplanted to the greenhouse of the skies—to the garden of the heavenly paradise! We thought they were very sweet when we saw their beautiful buds opening here with us. And so they were. But what should we think if we could see them now, as they are blooming and flourishing in the Saviour's garden above? Let me give you a few samples of these gathered flowers which Jesus has taken to Himself.

I was reading the other day of a little boy, only two years old, who had been taught to put up his baby-hands and offer his little prayer to Jesus. When dying, he looked at his father and said, 'By by, pa; baby going to sleep;' and then he shut his little eyes, never to open them again till the angel's trumpet shall waken him.

There was another little boy, three years old, who was just sinking into the arms of death. He said to his father, who was standing by his side, 'Father, there is beyond the sky a heaven of joy and love!'

There was another, a blind boy, who looked up as he was dying, and said, 'I see a light; it's heaven—it's heaven!'

There was a little Sunday-school boy who, when taken sick, was at first afraid to die. Turning to his mother, he said: 'The valley of death is very dark: mother, won't you go with me?' His poor mother couldn't say a word; she could only burst into tears. The little fellow then put his face towards the wall and prayed. Presently he turned to his sorrowing mother with a sweet look, and said : ' Mother, the valley isn't dark now, for Jesus is with me. I can go now.' And then he died.

Little Annie T. died when she was three years and three months old. On her deathbed she called for her father. When he came to her bedside she said : ' Pray—read.' 'What shall I read?' asked her father. 'About Jesus,' was her reply. When he had finished, she said, 'Sing, sing of Jesus.' When they stopped, she cried, ' More, more of Jesus.' And as she sank in death the words which they heard lingering in whispers on her lips were, ' Jesus, Jesus !'

James B. Jones died when he was nine years old. Before he died, he said to his parents : ' I am so happy I know not what to do. God loves me, and has pardoned all my sins for Jesus' sake. Who would have thought that God would be so kind to such a little boy as I am? Oh, I am so happy—I am so happy !' And thus Jesus gathered this sweet flower to Himself.

I might go on for ever so long giving you samples of these gathered flowers which Jesus has taken to Himself. All these that I have spoken of thus far have been gathered from other parts of our Saviour's garden. If there were time, I could tell you of many dear young flowers that Jesus has gathered from my own part of the Sunday-school garden. And every faithful minister of Jesus could do the same. The names of many sweet children who have glorified Jesus in their happy deaths are fresh in our memories.

And then how many, younger than these, baby-flowers, just in the bud, Jesus has gathered from our gardens! These were too young to be in school; but they belonged to Jesus, and He has gathered them to Himself. I think I see them now, with their sweet angel-like faces, as we took our last look before the coffin lid was screwed down upon them. But they are all with Jesus now. They are flowers which He has taken from our garden down here, to have them near Himself in heaven.

Jesus comes into His garden to *watch the growth of the flowers—to enjoy the beauty of the flowers—and to gather the flowers to Himself.*

Now let us see if we can recollect the important parts of this sermon. The text is in Cant. v. 1, 'I am come into my garden.' The sermon is about JESUS COMING INTO HIS GARDEN. We have considered the Sunday-school as the garden of Jesus. And then we had *two questions: Why is the Sunday-school like a garden? And what does Jesus come into it for?*

In answering the first question, we said the Sunday-school is like a garden *because of what is done for it. It is fenced—and weeded—the soil is improved—seeds and plants are put into it—and it is watered and cared for.*

The Sunday-school is like a garden also because of what grows in it, viz. *flowers and fruits.*

In answering the other question, we said *that Jesus comes into His garden to watch the growth of the flowers —to enjoy the beauty of the flowers—and to gather the flowers to Himself.*

Now, my dear children, there are two things I wish you especially to remember in connection with this subject. *Remember what God expects us to do for others.* God expects us to get others into His garden. How many children there are in our own land, and in other lands, who have no Sunday-school, no Bibles, no teachers. They are not in God's garden. They are out in the broad common of the world. God wants us to help to bring them into His garden. And when we make our offerings to send the Bible to those children and have them taught and cared for, then we are doing just what God desires us to do. You know our Saviour said to His disciples, 'Freely ye have received, freely give.' And He says the same to us. Then let us be very thankful to Him for bringing us into His garden, and let us try all we can to bring others in also. This is what God expects us to do for others. Remember this.

And then remember too what God expects us to do for

ourselves. He expects us to take good care of our part of the garden. Every one of you, my dear children, has a bed in God's garden to take care of. Your own heart is that bed. Oh, be sure that you take good care of it. Put plenty of good seed in it. Be careful in reading and trying to understand God's Word. That is the good seed. And be careful to keep the weeds out of your garden bed. Remember if you give way to proud feelings—or peevish, fretful, angry feelings; if you are selfish, or untruthful, or disobedient, then you are letting great ugly weeds spring up and grow in your part of God's garden. Watch for the weeds, oh, watch for the weeds! Pull them up at once! Don't let them stay a moment after you find them. And pray God for Jesus' sake to keep the weeds from growing in your hearts. Prayer has a wonderful power to keep those weeds from growing.

I was reading lately of a dear little girl who had a cross little brother. One day he struck his sister. His mother was going to punish him for it. But Mary his sister said, 'Please, mother, don't punish him; I think I can teach him not to strike me again.' She took him out of the room. Her mother went after them to see what she would do. Mary went with him into another room and closed the door. Then she made him kneel down by a chair, and she knelt by his side, and offered this sweet, simple prayer over him, 'O Lord, forgive my little brother for striking me. Give him a new heart that he may not strike me any more; and if he does strike me, or push me, put it into my heart not to strike him back, but to say, "Don't do so, little brother." Lord, hear me for Jesus' sake. Amen!' Ah, that little girl knew how to keep the weeds out of her garden-bed. Follow her example. Then your garden will flourish, and Jesus will look on it and come into it with pleasure.

VI.

The Ways of Doing Good.

'*Jesus . . . went about doing good.*'—ACTS x. 38.

WHAT a beautiful description this is of the life of Jesus! When we hear of any great man we always want to know how he lived, and what he used to do. General Washington was a great man, and all the young people in this country like to read or hear about him. We don't get tired of the interesting stories told of him. We like to hear of the boy George Washington,—about the hatchet and the cherry tree,—and how he wouldn't tell a lie. We like to hear about his giving up being a midshipman, when he wanted to be one so very much, because he was unwilling to do anything that would make his mother feel unhappy. We like to read about George Washington when a young colonel fighting the Indians, and how the Indian warrior took aim at him ever so many times in one day, and tried to kill him, but found he couldn't do it. And we like to read of Washington, the commander-in-chief of the American armies in the darkest days of the Revolutionary war, when he used to go all alone by himself in the snow-covered woods, and kneel down and pray that God would show him what to do, and help him to save the country.

And then there was Benjamin Franklin, the great philosopher,—and Christopher Columbus, the great

THE WAYS OF DOING GOOD.

discoverer,—and Peter the Great of Russia,—and Alfred the Great of England, and multitudes of other distinguished men. We like to read about them, and find out how they used to live, *because* they were great men. But you may put these, and all the other great men that ever lived, all together, and yet, when you come to compare them with Jesus, they are only just like one of the tiniest little stars you see shining in the sky at night when compared with the sun. Jesus was the wisest, and the best, and the greatest man that ever lived. He was *God* as well as man. He lived on earth not for Himself, but for us. He lived on earth for you and me. He came to do good to you and me, as well as to the Jews who lived 1800 years ago. Oh, surely then it is worth while for us to think and talk about Him!

'Jesus . . . went about doing good.' This needs no explanation. It is very plain and simple. Why, I suppose every one of these infant-school children knows what it means to 'go about doing good.' 'Jesus . . . went about doing good,' because He loved to do good, and because He was so able to do it. *He* could do good as no one else in the world ever could. He hadn't much money; for though He made the world, and all things in it, yet when He was here on earth He was so poor that He said, 'The foxes have holes, and the birds of the air have nests, but the Son of Man hath not where to lay His head.' But though He had no money to give away, He could do good in hundreds of other ways. He could heal the sick, whatever their diseases were. He could make the blind see, and the deaf hear, and the lame walk. He could raise the dead to life again in a moment. He could feed thousands of people with two or three small loaves of bread, and then have more bread left when they were done than there was before they began.

But there is another reason why 'Jesus . . . went about doing good.' He did it *to show us how to live.* We read in one place in the New Testament that He

'left us an example that we should follow His steps.'—
1 Pet. ii. 21. 'Jesus . . . went about doing good,' in
order to show you and me, and all people, how we ought
to live. And this is what I wish to talk to you about
this afternoon. When you go home from church, if
anybody asks you what was the sermon about, tell them
it was about *the best ways of doing good*. I wish to speak
to you about *four* ways in which we should all try to
be doing good.

The first way in which we should try to do good is by
BECOMING CHRISTIANS OURSELVES.

True Christians are the most useful people in the
world. They are doing good all the time. You know
that many of our houses and other large buildings have
iron-rods running from above the top of the chimney
along the sides of the building down into the ground.
What are those rods called? Lightning-rods. Often,
when thunderstorms come up, we hear of houses being
struck by lightning. Sometimes these houses are very
much injured, and the people living in them are killed.
Those lightning-rods are intended to protect the houses.
They carry the lightning off into the ground and prevent it from doing any harm. Lightning-rods are very
useful things. And true Christians are like lightning-rods.
When God is angry with wicked people for their sins, He
is often kept from punishing them on account of the
good Christians—the praying people—who live among
them.

You remember reading in the Bible about Sodom and
Gomorrha. The inhabitants of those cities were so
wicked that God said He would destroy them. Abraham
prayed for those cities because he had a nephew, Lot,
living there. He asked God to be pleased not to destroy
them, if He found ten righteous persons there; and God
promised that He would not, if He found that many
good people there. But Lot was the only good man
found there. So Lot was sent away, and then those
guilty cities were burned up. If there had been ten

THE WAYS OF DOING GOOD. 93

Christians in Sodom, they would have acted like lightning-rods to those cities, and have saved them.

You know how useful the light is which shines out from the sun. Well, Jesus compares Christians to the light. He said to His disciples, 'Ye are the light of the world.' If we were travelling along a dangerous road, full of pits and precipices, the light would be very useful to show us where the road lay, and how we might keep out of the pits along the road. Now, in living in this world, we are travelling along a road that is full of dangers. But true Christians are the only ones who can see these dangers, and know how to avoid them. God teaches them this by His blessed Spirit. And for this reason they are compared to the *light*. And if we would be like lights in the world, showing people the dangers that are about them, and how they may escape those dangers, and get to heaven at last, then we must become true Christians. This means that we must have our wicked hearts changed, and learn to love Jesus, and be like Him. To be a Christian is to be like Jesus. Being baptized and belonging to the Church won't make us true Christians, unless our hearts are changed, and we are taught to love Jesus. And we never can begin to do good in the right way until we become Christians ourselves. Here, for instance, is a watch. A watch is a very useful thing. It is useful to tell the time of day. The inside of the watch is full of works. In the midst of these works is what is called the mainspring. It is the mainspring which makes the watch go and keep good time. But suppose the mainspring of my watch is broken, will it keep time? No. Well, then, if I want my watch to go about with me 'doing good,' or being useful, what must I do with it? Take it to the watch-maker, and get a new mainspring put in it. But you and I are just like a watch. Our hearts are like the mainspring. A wicked heart is like a broken mainspring. If you have a wicked heart, a heart that has not been changed, you cannot begin to be useful, or to 'go about doing good' in the right way. You must take your heart to Jesus, and ask Him to change it; to give you a new heart; to put a new mainspring in the broken watch of your soul. Then it will be ready to keep time, to do good, or to be useful in the right way. And you need not wait till you grow up to be men and women before you do this. You may do it now.

One day a lady was teaching a class of little girls in Sunday-school. She was talking to them about the very thing of which I am now speaking to you. 'My dear children,' she said, 'how soon may we give our hearts to God, and become true Christians?' They didn't answer at first. Then she spoke to them one by one. Turning to the oldest scholar in the class, she asked, 'What do you say, Mary?'

'When we are thirteen.'

'What do you say, Jane?'

'When we are ten.'

'What do you say, Susan?'

'When we are six.'

At last she came to little Lillie, the youngest scholar in the class.

'Well, Lillie,' she said, 'and how soon do you think we may give our hearts to God?'

'Just as soon as we feel that we are sinners, and know who God is!' said Lillie.

How beautiful an answer that was! and how true! Yes, 'as soon as you feel that you are a sinner and know who God is,' you may give Him your heart, and become a Christian.

This is the first way in which we should try to be doing good, by becoming Christians ourselves.

But the second way in which we are to do good, is by TRYING TO MAKE OTHERS CHRISTIANS.

Suppose you were travelling through a hot, sandy desert with a company of friends. You have no water, and are almost perishing from thirst. You separate from one another, and go in different directions

THE WAYS OF DOING GOOD.

searching for water. Presently you find a spring of clear, cool, beautiful water. You kneel down and take a nice long drink. And then what would be the next thing you would do? Why, at the top of your voice you would cry out—'Water!—water! Come this way;—here is water!' You would want your friends to come and drink of the water that had refreshed you. And this is just the way we should feel when we become Christians ourselves. We should want to have our friends and others become Christians too. We should feel just as the little heathen girl did in England. She had been taken from the island of New Zealand to England with the children of some missionaries to be educated. While there she became a Christian. Before this she was so pleased with living in England that she didn't care about going back to her own country. But as soon as she learned to love Jesus, she became very anxious to go home; and when some of her friends tried to persuade her to stay where she was, she said: 'Do you think I can keep the good news to myself? No; I want to go home and tell my friends there about Jesus.'

She was trying to do good in this *second way* that we are now speaking of.

Some time ago an old man gave his heart to Jesus and became a Christian. Soon after this he began to think how he could make himself useful and be doing good. He had a great many friends who were very wicked men. He was very anxious that these should become Christians too. He made out a list of the names of his old associates. When he had finished this list, and counted it over, he found that it contained one hundred and sixteen names. Some of these were infidels, some were drunkards, and some were among the worst men in the town where he lived. He began to pray for these people. He talked to them when he had an opportunity, and gave them tracts and good books to read. Some refused to listen to him, and others made fun of him; but still he went on praying

and working for them, and trying to do them good.
And what was the result? Why, within two years from
the time when that old man became a Christian—*one
hundred* of the persons whose names were on his list had
become Christians too! That was doing good indeed!

A Christian gentleman was travelling on a steamboat.
He took some tracts out and scattered them about for
the passengers to read. Many were glad to get them,
and read them carefully. But one gentleman was there
who disliked religion and religious people very much.
He took one of the tracts and doubled it up, and then
deliberately took out his pen-knife and cut it all up into
little pieces. He then held up his hand and scattered
the pieces over the side of the boat, to show his
contempt for religion. When he had done this he saw
one of the pieces sticking to his coat. He picked it off
and looked at it a moment before throwing it away.
On one side of that bit of paper was only one word.
It was the word—'*God.*' He turned it over; on the other
side was the word—'Eternity.' He threw away the bit
of paper; he got rid of that easily enough; but those
two solemn words—'God' and 'Eternity'—he could not
get rid of. He tried drinking—he tried gambling—to
drive those words from his mind, but it was of no use.
They haunted him wherever he went, and he never had
any comfort till he became a Christian. That little
piece of paper with those two words upon it was the
means of his conversion.

But now let me tell you a story to show you how a
Sunday-school scholar may do good in the way of which
I am speaking. Little Mary was a Sunday-school
scholar. Her mother was dead, and she tried to take
her place in the family as much as she could. Her
father never went to church, but to Mary's great grief
was getting into the way of going to the tavern at night,
and would sometimes come home drunk. Mary had a
very kind and faithful Sunday-school teacher. Through
God's blessing on her prayers and teaching, Mary became

a Christian. She had always loved her father, but now she loved him more than ever. She was very anxious that he should become a Christian. But what could she do? She knew if she should speak to him about it, he would be very angry. After thinking and praying over it a great deal, she took a slip of paper and wrote upon it—'Papa, won't you be a Christian?' This she left upon the table in his room. In the morning when he got up it was almost the first thing that met his eyes. He read it over—'Papa, won't you be a Christian?' He tore it in little pieces, and throwing it on the floor, stamped on it with his feet.

Mary was sorry, but she didn't give up. The next night she wrote again—'Papa, *do* be a Christian!' and left it in the same place. Her father read it. He was angry, but did not tear it as before; he put it in his pocket and went out. All that day the words were ringing in his ears—'Papa, *do* be a Christian.' They made him think of his mother and the prayers she taught him, and his heart began to soften. That night Mary wrote on another slip of paper—'Papa, won't you be a Christian?—tell Mary.' In the morning she was up very early, and busy about the breakfast, but listening with a beating heart to the sounds that came from her father's room. She heard the bit of paper rustle in his hands, and then these words—'Mary!—where are you, Mary?' In a moment she was sobbing in her father's arms, with her face close to his, feeling I cannot tell you how happy. That was the beginning of a great change in her home. Her father soon became a Christian. Mary was a feeble little girl, yet she was the means of doing a great deal of good.

The second way of doing good is by trying to make others Christians.

The third way of doing good is by HELPING THE SICK AND POOR.

When Jesus was on earth, while ready to do good to all men, He was always especially ready to help the poor.

He kept company with them more than with the rich. He did everything in His power to help and comfort them. He told His disciples that whenever they did a kindness to one of His poor He would consider it as done to Himself. He said that even 'a cup of cold water' given to one of them would be remembered and rewarded by Him. And the Apostle James tells us that a great part of true religion consists in 'visiting the fatherless and widows,' that means the poor and the sick, 'in their affliction,' and in trying to help and comfort them. How singular it is that we find poor people everywhere! God might have made the world without having poor people in it. But He thought it best to have poor people. He says in the Bible—'I will leave in the midst of you an afflicted and poor people.' One reason why God does this is, that we might have an opportunity of 'doing good' by trying to help and comfort the poor and afflicted. And this is a work that every one can help in. Young people are apt to think that it is only their fathers and mothers, and persons who are grown up, who can do good by visiting and helping poor and sick people. But this is a great mistake. Children can do good in this way as well as grown-up people.

Let me tell you what good a little girl did in the way of which I am now speaking, and then you can see what you may do if you are willing to try.

Mary Parsons was a bright, happy little girl. And the reason why she was so happy was that she was always trying to do good to somebody. One day a lady, who lived in their neighbourhood, called in to see Mary's mother. This lady had just been visiting a poor old woman who lived not far off from them, and she stepped in to talk about her. The poor old woman was eighty-six years old. She lived by herself in a dark, damp cellar. She had no money and no relatives, and had nothing to live on but what the kind neighbours sent in to her from time to time. Mary listened with great interest while the lady was speaking, and then she said,

'O mother, please let me carry her over some breakfast and dinner every day : we have so much left, much more than she could eat.' Mary was so earnest about it that her mother said she might do it. And there you might have seen this little girl, after breakfast and after dinner each day, filling a small basket with nice things from the table, and carrying them down the street to old Mrs. Gordon. Many a fine apple and peach, and plum and pear, she slipped into the basket for the poor old woman.

No matter how anxious her little sisters were for Mary to play with them ; no matter whether it was hot or cold, wet or dry, Mary never got tired, and never forgot to have the breakfast and dinner ready for her old friend. Sometimes she would take the Bible and read some of its beautiful chapters; for the poor woman was almost blind, and to hear God's precious Word read was a great comfort to her. Sometimes Mary would take her doll's frocks and sit down by her side, and chat away merrily to amuse her.

And how do you suppose old Mrs. Gordon felt towards this dear child for all her kindness? When she was speaking about her one day her eyes filled with tears as she said, 'Oh, she brings a ray of sunshine with her every time she comes, and it seems to brighten my dark room long after she is gone. God bless her! She is one of the dear lambs of Jesus, I am sure.'

Now you see how beautifully Mary was doing good in this *third* way that I am speaking of. Yet Mary Parsons was only eight years old when she began to do this. Is there no poor old woman, or sick and hungry child, in your neighbourhood, to whom you can take food from your table that would not be missed? 'Jesus went about doing good.' See if you can't follow His example in this *third way, by helping the sick and poor.*

The fourth and last way of doing good of which I would speak is, BY BEING KIND TO ALL.

Jesus was all the time speaking kind words and doing kind things. See, there He is entering into a city called

Nain. As He draws near there is a funeral coming out. The dead person is a young man, 'the only son of his mother, and she is a widow.' Ah! how sad and sorrowful she feels as she follows her darling boy to the grave! How lonely she will feel when she goes back to her empty house! Her heart is almost broken. Jesus knows how she feels. He pities her. With a kind and tender voice He says to her, 'Weep not.' But how can she help weeping when her only son is dead? Jesus knows this. So He stops the funeral. He goes up to the corpse and says, 'Young man, I say unto thee, Arise.' In a moment he opens his eyes. He gets up, and Jesus gives him back alive to the arms of his rejoicing mother. Ah! that was doing good indeed! We can't do good in that way, true, but we can do good by kindness in many ways.

One day a gentleman saw two boys going along one of the streets in New York. They were barefooted. Their clothes were ragged and dirty, and tied together by pieces of string. One of the boys was perfectly happy over a half-withered bunch of flowers which he had just picked up in the street. 'I say, Billy,' said he to his companion, 'wasn't somebody real good to drop these 'ere posies jest where I could find them—and they're so pooty and nice? Look sharp, Billy, mebby you'll find something bimeby.' Presently the gentleman heard his merry voice again saying, 'Oh jolly! Billy, if here ain't 'most half a peach, and 'tain't mush dirty neither. 'Cause you hain't found nothin' you may bite first.' Billy was just going to take a very little taste of it, when his companion said, '*Bite bigger, Billy*, mebby we'll find another 'fore long.' What a noble heart that poor boy had in spite of his rags and dirt! He was 'doing good' in the fourth way that we are speaking of. There was nobody for him to be kind to but his companion in poverty—the poor ragged boy at his side. But he was showing him all the kindness in his power when he said, 'Bite bigger, Billy.' There was nothing greedy, nothing selfish about that boy.

THE WAYS OF DOING GOOD.

His conduct shows us how even a poor ragged beggar boy can do good by showing kindness.

'Bite bigger, Billy,—mebby we'll find another 'fore long.' Who can help admiring the noble heart of that poor boy? I would rather have that boy's kind and generous spirit than have a monarch's crown upon my head without it. 'Bite bigger, Billy;' think of these words if you are ever tempted to be unkind or selfish to your companions.

I remember reading not long ago about a man and his wife who were known to live very unhappily together. They were said to be the most quarrelsome people in the whole village in which they lived. They wouldn't bear the least thing from each other. Like a cat and dog, there was a constant snarling, and growling, and quarrelling between them. But all at once it was observed by some of their neighbours that a great change had passed over them. They didn't quarrel any more. No harsh, cross words passed between them. Instead of this, they were observed to be gentle and kind to each other, and their house, from being a scene of constant strife, became the home of peace and happiness. Of course this excited a good deal of surprise in the neighbourhood. Everybody was wondering what had happened to old Mr. and Mrs. Snarling.

At last an old lady in the neighbourhood, whom we may call Miss Inquisitive, felt that she couldn't stand it any longer. She must find out what it was. So she paid a visit to their house and said, 'Mrs. Snarling, everybody in the village is talking about the wonderful change which has come over you and your husband. But nobody seems to know what it's owing to; so I thought I would just come in and ask you what it is which has produced this change.'

'I am glad to see you, Miss Inquisitive,' said Mrs. Snarling; 'the change, I assure you, has been a very happy one to us. It has been brought about by *two bears*.'

'Two bears!' exclaimed Miss Inquisitive, lifting up her hands in astonishment.

'Yes, two bears; and I'm very glad they ever came into our house.'

'But what in nature do you mean?'

'I mean two Scripture bears.'

'Two *Scripture* bears! why, you puzzle me more and more.'

'It's true, though.'

'I don't remember reading in Scripture of any two bears, except those that ate up the wicked children who mocked the Prophet Elisha; and they must have been dead long ago.'

'Yes; but there are two other bears mentioned in Scripture.'

'Pray tell me where they are spoken of, for I'm sure I don't recollect 'em.'

'We read about one of them in Gal. vi. 2, where it says, "Bear ye one another's burdens." And we read about the other in Eph. iv. 2, where it says, "Forbearing one another in love." Their names are—Bear and Forbear.'

'Well, I'm sure!' said Miss Inquisitive, and away she went home.

The simple meaning of it was that Mr. and Mrs. Snarling had become Christians, and had taken these two Scripture bears home to live with them. How I wish you would all take these two bears home with you this afternoon! Yes, and keep them there. Let them stay in the nursery—in the dining-room—in the chamber where you sleep—and in the playroom. Take them with you when you go to school—make them your companions wherever you go. They make no noise. They cost nothing to keep. They can do no harm, but they may do a great deal of good. Oh, if these two bears were only allowed to come into every house and dwell there, how much trouble and sorrow it would prevent! and how much good it would do!

THE WAYS OF DOING GOOD.

Now we have spoken of four ways in which we may do good:—*by becoming Christians ourselves; by trying to make others Christians; by helping the sick and poor, and by being kind to all.*

'Jesus went about doing good.' Let us all pray that God may give us grace to become like Him. We may make a suitable prayer for this subject out of the words of the hymn which leads us to look to Jesus, and say—

> 'Thy fair example may we trace,
> To teach us what we ought to be;
> Make us, by Thy transforming grace,
> Dear Saviour, daily more like Thee!'

VII.

The Blessedness of Giving.

'Jesus . . . said, It is more blessed to give than to receive.'—
ACTS xx. 35.

UR last text told us what Jesus *did*. He 'went about doing good.' Our text to-day tells us what Jesus *said*. He said, 'It is more blessed to give than to receive.' It is very pleasant to hear people talk about things with which we know that they are well acquainted; but if a person attempts to speak to us on some subject which we are sure beforehand that he knows nothing at all about—why, nobody wants to hear him. Suppose some one should give notice that he was going to deliver a lecture about the way in which houses are built in the moon, would you care about going to hear him? No. And why not? You would say at once, 'The man doesn't know anything about that.' But suppose that the great explorer, Dr. Kane, after he had spent two winters up towards the North Pole, should have given notice that he was going to lecture about the Polar regions, shouldn't we all have been very anxious to go and hear him? Yes, for we should say, 'He has been there himself, and he knows all about those regions.' We like to hear people speak of things which we are sure that they understand.

Well, when Jesus said, 'It is more blessed to give

than to receive,' did He understand what He was speaking about? Yes, He understood it well. He knew all about it. And everything that Jesus said was true. And nothing was ever more true than these words of our text. Some people don't believe that it is more blessed to give than to receive; but Jesus says it is so, and He knows best.

Our sermon to-day will be about *the blessedness of giving*.

I wish to give you *three reasons* why it is more blessed to give than to receive. The first reason is—THAT IT IS MORE LIKE GOD.

God is the greatest of all givers. It tells us in one place in the Bible that He is 'the giver of *every good* and perfect gift.' It tells us in another place that He 'giveth to all life and breath and all things.' Who gave us our hands to work with? God. Who gave us our feet to walk with? God. Who gave us our ears to hear, and our tongues to talk with? God. Who gave us our minds to think, and our hearts to love with? God. Who gave us these lungs to breathe with? God. And who gives us the air, fresh and good, which we are breathing through these lungs all the time? God. We wake up every morning and find the beautiful light coming into our windows;—who gives us the light? God. Yes, God has been giving light to the world for six thousand years, and in all that time He has never stopped giving for a single moment. We sit down to our tables three times a day when we are hungry, and there is good nourishing food for us to eat. Who gives us that food? God. We go out in the summer time to take a long walk. The sun is hot, and the road is dusty. After a while we become very thirsty. Our tongues are parched, our throats are dry; we long for a drink of water. Presently we come to a spring. There is a shady dell by the roadside. Beautiful green moss covers the rocks around the spring. At the foot of the rocks is a large, natural basin of clear, cool, crystal water. In the middle of the basin we see the fountain bubbling up through the clean white sand and little pebbles at the bottom. We stoop down and drink. How cool! how sweet! how refreshing it is! Who gives us this nice cool water? God. Yes, God gives us our health—our strength—our clothes—our friends—our teachers—our parents—our homes—our churches—our ministers—our Bibles. We cannot mention a single thing we have that is necessary for us, or that helps to make us comfortable, that does not come from God. The Bible tells us that God ' gives us richly *all things* to enjoy.'

I was reading lately of a little boy who was trying to be like God by being a giver. He loved to give. He would go to his father sometimes half-a-dozen times in a day, with his bright eye sparkling, and his little round face all in a glow, and say, ' Pa, I want a penny to give to a poor beggar at the door,' or 'to the organ-grinder,' or 'to the little girl that wants cold victuals.' And then on Sunday mornings he would come and ask for something for the Sunday-school Missionary Society, and for many other things. His father wanted him to form the habit of giving while he was young, and so he always let him have what he wanted for these good objects.

But one day, when he came to ask for something, his father said to him, ' My son, don't you think you give away a great deal of money?'

'Why, yes, pa,' said he, 'and I do so love to give.'

'But then you come to *me* for all you give. It's not *your own* money that you are so liberal with.'

This seemed to be a new thought to the little fellow, and he turned away to his play, perplexed a little by what his father had said to him. Presently, however, he came running back.

' Papa,' he asked, 'who gives you the money that you give away?'

' I earn it by hard labour, my son.'

' But who gives you strength to labour with, pa?' asked the little fellow.

THE BLESSEDNESS OF GIVING.

'God gives us our strength,' said his father.

'And, pa, haven't you often told me that God gives us everything?'

'Yes, my son, every good thing we have God gives us.'

'Well, pa, I love to give away the money you give me; *don't you love to give away the money God gives you?*'

The father hugged the little prattler in his arms and kissed him, gave him what he wanted, and let him go. And then that father sat down to think over the question which his dear child had asked him. Like a great many other people, he had forgotten that the money which he had was not his own, but God's. All the money in the world belongs to God. In one place in the Bible God says, 'The gold is mine, and the silver is mine.'—Hag. ii. 8. God doesn't give us money to keep: He only *lends* it to us, to use for Him, and to do good with it. And when we die He will call us to give Him an account of the use we have made of it. God loves to give, and He loves to have His people give. God is such a wonderful Giver, that when He found we couldn't be saved, or be happy in any other way, 'He gave His only begotten Son' to die for us. And when we learn to give, and love to give, we become like God in this respect.

'It is more blessed to give than to receive,' then, because *it is more like God.*

This is our first reason.

The second reason is that it is MORE USEFUL. We can do more good by giving than by receiving. Suppose God should stop giving for just one day, what would be the consequence? We should all die. Everything would perish. The world, the whole universe, would go to ruin. Only think, then, how useful it is to us that God is a giver! *Giving is more useful* TO OURSELVES than receiving, and *it is more useful to* OTHERS *too.*

Now everybody will admit that it is more useful to others to give than to receive; but that it is more useful to *ourselves*, as well as to others, may not appear quite so plain. Yet it is true.

For instance, suppose I want to have my arm become very strong. I ask one of my friends what is the best way to make my arm strong. He says to me, 'Carry it in a sling, and don't use it at all. When you use your arm you waste its strength, and the more you use it the weaker it will get. But if you carry it in a sling without using it, it will become stronger every day.' Well, I take his advice. I put my arm in a sling, and don't use it for anything. But I find, after a while, that my arm is growing thinner and weaker all the time. Its strength is wasting away every day. This won't do. Then I ask another friend how I shall make my arm strong. He gives me advice the very opposite of what the other gave me. He says, 'Take your arm out of that sling. Go to work at sawing, or splitting wood. Use your arm all you can. The more you use it properly the stronger it will grow. Look at that blacksmith! He is wielding that heavy hammer all the time, and see what an arm of strength he has got!'

I take this friend's advice. I throw away the sling, and use my arm all I can. And now I find my arm growing stronger every day. Proper exercise for the arm is the best way to make it strong.

And what is true of the arm is true of the heart too. Our hearts will grow larger, and stronger, and better, by proper exercise. And what do you suppose is the proper exercise for the heart? Why, *giving*. If we are not in the habit of giving, our hearts have no proper exercise. We are carrying them in a sling. *A good many people carry their hearts in a sling all their lives.* And the consequence is that their hearts grow narrow and little, and good for nothing. They become shrivelled and dried. If they would begin to exercise their hearts by giving, they would find that what Jesus said is true: 'It *is* more blessed to give than to receive.' *It is more useful to ourselves.* Did you ever hear the fable of

The Selfish Pool and the Liberal Spring? This illustrates the point before us so nicely, that I must bring it in here.

There was a little spring or fountain away up among the mountains. It sent out a little stream of water, and said to it, 'Now hurry down the mountain's side, and pour this water into the river that flows through yonder plain.' Away went the stream, shining like a silver thread, and sparkling like a diamond, as it hurried on to bear its water to the river. Presently the stream passed by a stagnant pool. 'Halloo! Mister Streamlet,' cried the pool, 'where are you going in such a hurry?'

'I'm going to the river to carry it this water which God has given me.'

'You're a very silly creature,' said the pool. 'Don't you know that the summer will be here by and by, and if you give away your water now, when the hot sun shines upon you you'll dry up and perish.'

'Well,' said the streamlet, 'if I am to die so soon, I had better work while the day lasts. If I am likely to lose this treasure from the heat, I had better do good with it while I have it. Good-bye, Miss Pool,' said the stream, and away it went, blessing and rejoicing everything in its course.

The pool smiled at what she considered the folly of the stream, and said to herself, 'You silly creature! I won't part with a drop of my water, but will keep it all for my own use when the hot days of summer come.'

Presently the heat of summer came, and fell upon that little stream. But the trees crowded to its brink, and threw their sheltering branches over it, for it had brought life and refreshment to them. The sun peeped through the branches and smiled upon its dimpled face, seeming to say, 'Oh, I won't hurt you!' The little birds sipped its silver tide, and sang its praises; the flowers breathed their fragrance on its bosom; and the beasts of the field loved to linger by its banks; and thus it went on blessing and blessed of all.

But what about the prudent, selfish pool? It didn't believe that 'it is more blessed to give than to receive.' It kept its waters. It became stagnant and unhealthy The water grew thick and disagreeable. A green scum gathered on the surface of it. Neither the birds nor beasts would drink of it. Even the frogs hopped away from it; and as the sun grew hotter and hotter, it dried up altogether.

But did the little stream dry up? Oh, no! God took care of that. It carried its water to the river. The river bore it to the sea. The sun shone upon the sea, and warmed it. The vapours rose from its surface and formed clouds. The clouds floated away and emptied themselves in rain upon the mountains. The little fountain was kept supplied, and though it gave away its water so freely, it never dried up. What a beautiful illustration this fable affords of the truth and meaning of our Saviour's words when He said, 'It is more blessed to give than to receive.' *It is so because it is more useful. It is more useful to ourselves.*

But it is more useful to others as well as to ourselves.

If we keep our money without using it, what good will it do either to ourselves or others? There was once a Scottish nobleman whose name and title was Lord Braco. He was very rich, but very miserly. He kept his own accounts himself, instead of having a steward to keep them, like other rich men, because he was unwilling to pay the salary of a steward. All the money he got he had changed into gold and silver, which he kept locked up in great iron chests in a strong vault. He was so close and stingy about money, that one day when a farmer who rented a farm from him came to pay his rent, the money he brought was just *one farthing* short, and would you believe it? he made the man go all the way back to his home, a distance of several miles, and get that farthing before he would give him a receipt.

Well, when it was all settled the farmer said, 'Now,

Braco, I'll give you a shilling if you'll let me see all the silver and gold you've got.'

'Agreed,' said the miserly lord. Then he took him into his vault and opened the great iron chests full of gold and silver, so that he could see it all. Then the farmer gave him the promised shilling, and said, 'Now, Braco, I'm as rich as you are.'

'Ay, mon,' said his lordship, 'and how can that be?'

'Because *I've looked* at your gold and silver, and that is all you will ever do with it.'

The farmer was right. Lord Braco's gold and silver would do no good, either to himself or any one else, while it was locked up unused.

Now let us take an example of a different kind. Some years ago the teachers of a certain Sunday-school were making up a box of things to send to a missionary station in India. The scholars of the school were invited to bring anything they had to give and put it in the box. One poor little girl in the school was very anxious to send something in the box. But all she had in the world to give was a single penny. She resolved to give this. She bought a tract with that penny, and gave the tract to her teacher to put in the box. It was put in. The box went across the great ocean. It was opened at a missionary station at Burdwan, in India. That tract fell into the hands of the son of one of the chiefs of Burdwan. The reading of that tract led him to become a Christian. Then he was very anxious that others should become Christians too. He began to talk about Jesus in his family. He distributed tracts and Christian books round about in the neighbourhood where he lived. Being a young man of great influence, his example had a wonderful effect. In one year *fifteen hundred* of the natives of that part of the country gave up their idolatry, were baptized, and became Christians, through the labours of that young prince. And all this good resulted from the one tract bought by that poor little girl's single penny. Now think of all this good being done by one penny, and then think of all Lord Braco's gold and silver lying useless, and you must admit that it *is* more blessed to give than to receive or keep. It is *more useful.*

But the third reason why it is more blessed to give than to receive is that there is MORE HAPPINESS *in it.*

One of the great secrets of being happy is to be doing good, or trying to make others happy. But to do this we must learn to be givers. Here I have a nice story to show you how true this is.

Little Robert Manly was only about five years old. Yet young as he was he liked to have his own way. He thought a great deal about pleasing himself, and this is not at all the best way to be happy. A very poor family lived down the lane behind his mother's house. The father of this family was a drunkard. He was very cruel to his wife and children, and often beat them.

One day this poor woman came to Robert's mother to beg a little new milk for her sick baby. Mrs. Manly had none to spare except what she had saved for Robert's supper. 'But I will give the poor creature this,' she said, 'for Robert can do without his milk for once.' At supper time his mother told him how she had given away his milk for the poor sick baby. Robert didn't like this at all. He pouted and cried. He refused to eat his bread and butter, and kept muttering about the milk being *his*, and nobody else having any right to it.

His mother was very sorry to see him so selfish, and she lifted up her heart in prayer to God that He would take away these bad feelings, and make him a better boy. The next day she took Robert with her to see this poor family, thinking that the sight of their misery would do him good. So they went down the lane to visit the drunkard's family. How cold and forlorn everything seemed there! It made little Robert shiver to look round on that cheerless home. The poor woman thanked Mrs. Manly over and over again for the new milk. 'It kept the baby still all night,' she said; 'her father didn't beat her, for he beats her when he comes home drunk and finds her crying. Poor thing! she can't help it: she's hungry and wants something nourishing.'

'But I don't know as I can spare you any more,' said Robert's mother; 'I want to very much, but'—and she stopped.

'Oh!' said the woman, 'I know, I can't expect it every night; you're very good, and I'm very much obliged to you.'

'Is there anything else I could do for you?' asked Robert's mother.

'Nothing, thank you, now; the most is a drop of new milk,' she said, sighing, and kissing her poor sick baby.

As they walked home, Robert didn't say a word, though he was generally very talkative. He seemed to be thinking earnestly about something. His mother said nothing, but prayed in her heart that God would teach him to feel and do what was right. At supper time Robert's bowl of milk was set by his plate. He did not come to the table, but sat looking in the fire.

'Come, Robert,' said his father.

He obeyed, but gently shoved his bowl of milk on one side. In a few minutes he went to his mother's side and said in a whisper:

'Mother, may I take my milk to the poor sick baby?'

'Yes, my son,' said his mother.

He went into the kitchen, and presently Mary, the girl, came in and carried out the milk. Nothing was seen of the little fellow for some time. By and by he came bounding into the room covered over with snow-flakes, and shouting cheerfully:

'Mother, the baby's got the milk. Mary and I took it to her. Now she'll sleep; won't she? Her mother said, "God bless you, my child!" that was to me; and, mother, my milk tastes very good to-night' (smacking his lips); 'I mean my *no milk*.'

Yes, little Robert was proving the truth of our Saviour's words, 'It is more blessed to give than to receive,' when he smacked his lips and said the '*no milk*' was better than the milk. It made him happier to give his milk to the poor sick baby than to drink it himself.

I want to give you *one* other illustration of this part of our sermon before I close.

There lived an old man in Germany named Gerard Steiner. He had three sons: Adolphus, the oldest; Henry, the second; and little Bernard, the youngest. One day he called the boys to him. He had an open letter in his hand, which he had just been reading.

'My dear boys,' said their father, 'this letter is from your kind Uncle Bernard. He is very ill. The doctor says he cannot live, and he has sent for me to come and see him before he dies. I shall probably be away all the summer. I hope you will be good boys while I am gone; and here is a message for you from your dying uncle. Listen to it attentively; he says, "Give a handful of grain to each of the three boys when you leave them to come to me, and tell them to do with it what they think best during your absence; and when you return you will decide who has made the best use of it, and will reward that one according as I shall tell you."'

Mr. Steiner then gave each boy his handful of grain, and started on his journey.

He was absent a long while. One day, at the close of summer, little Bernard stood watching at the open window. Presently a carriage drove up to the door, and an elderly gentleman got out, holding a small tin box in his hand.

'Oh, father's come! father's come!' cried Bernard. The boys all rushed out and threw their arms round their father's neck, and told him how glad they were to see him again after his long absence.

'And I am very glad to see you all looking so well, my dear boys,' said Mr. Steiner, as he stooped down and gave each of them a kiss.

Then they all entered the house. Mr. Steiner now placed the tin box that he held in his hand upon the

THE BLESSEDNESS OF GIVING.

table; and taking a small key from his pocket, opened it, and took out a piece of parchment, which contained the will of his brother, Bernard Steiner.

The boys looked on sorrowfully while their father, with trembling hand, unfolded the will and said:

'I had the sad pleasure, my dear boys, of being with your dear uncle when he died. He died a peaceful, happy death. In this, his last will, he leaves all his property to the one of you that I shall decide has made the best use of the handful of grain that I gave each of you before I left home. Now let me hear, my children, what you have done with it.'

'I,' said Adolphus, 'have saved mine. I put it in a small wooden box in a dry place, and it's just as fresh as the day that you gave it me.'

'My son,' said his father in a stern voice, 'you have laid by the grain, and what has it profited either yourself or any one else? Nothing. So it is with money; laid up, or kept, it does no good to any. *That* is not the right use to make of it.'

'Well, Henry,' said Mr. Steiner, turning to his next son, 'what have you done with your handful of grain?'

'I ground it to flour, father, and had a nice sweet cake made of it, which I have eaten.'

'Foolish boy!' he exclaimed; 'and now it's all gone. You used it for yourself alone; that was not the best use to make of the grain, neither is it the best use to make of money.' And then, drawing his youngest son to him, he said, 'What use has my little Bernard made of the handful of grain I gave him?'

The child smiled, and clasping his father's hand, said, 'Come with me, father, and I will show you.'

They all followed the boy as he led the way towards a field belonging to his father at some distance from the house.

'See, father,' exclaimed the happy child, 'I sowed my handful of grain in the earth, and there you see what has become of it,' pointing with delight to a corner of the field where the tall, slender grain was growing, laden with its golden ears, and waving and rustling beneath the gentle breeze.

The father smiled, and resting his hand upon the head of Bernard, said:

'You have done well, my son. You sowed the grain in the earth, and it has yielded a bountiful harvest. *This was the best use to make of it.* Your uncle's fortune belongs to you. Use it as wisely as you have the handful of grain. Don't lay it up, as Adolphus did. Don't use it for yourself alone, as Henry did. Use it freely for others; for the poor, for the widow and the fatherless, for the little ones of Christ, and He will remember it, and reward you abundantly, and you will find how true His own words were when He said, " It is more blessed to give than to receive."'

There is more happiness in giving than in receiving. Little Robert felt this when he gave his milk to the sick baby; and little Bernard felt the same when he sowed his handful of grain in the earth, instead of keeping it, or eating it, as his brothers had done.

Now we have had three reasons why it is more blessed to give than to receive. *The first reason is, that it is more like God. The second is, that it is more useful. The third is, that there is more happiness in it.*

And now, my dear young friends, I wonder how many of you really believe that these words of Jesus are true? If you do believe them, you will show it by learning to give. If you have money to give, give that. If you have no money, then you can set up to be givers without any money. You can give kind words. You can give kind actions. Jesus says, if you give 'a cup of cold water to one of the least of His people, you shall in no wise lose your reward.' Form the habit of giving while you are young, and it will be a great blessing to you all your life.

But there is one thing, especially, that God wants you to give to Him. It is something which each of you has,

THE BLESSEDNESS OF GIVING.

and each of you can give, if you will. God says, 'Give me thine heart.' 'It is more blessed to give' this to God, than to receive anything or everything the world contains. Who will make this gift to-day?

VIII.

Gathering the Fragments: Time and Knowledge.

'*Gather up the fragments . . . that nothing be lost.*'—JOHN vi. 12.

WHEN Jesus spoke these words, He had just been performing a great miracle. A vast congregation of five thousand people had collected around Him. Some of them had come from a great distance. They had heard Him preach, but were unwilling to go home as soon as the preaching is over. They wanted to stay and hear Him again. They had seen Him work miracles. He had healed the sick, opened the eyes of the blind, and made the lame whole, and they were anxious to stay and see more of His wonderful works performed. But they were away from their homes, tired and hungry. Jesus felt a pity for them. He resolved to give them something to eat. But when He inquired what provisions the disciples had, He found that five small loaves, a little bigger than rolls, and two little fishes, were all they had to spread before that multitude. These wouldn't have made a crumb apiece for one quarter of that congregation. But still, Jesus told His disciples to make the people sit down, and get ready for dinner, just as if He had a cartload of provisions. When they were all seated, Jesus asked a blessing on the food before them. Then He took one of the loaves, and began to break it up; but, as fast as He broke off a piece, the loaf from which He broke it would instantly grow out again as big as it was before. And it was the same with the fishes. The loaves and fishes grew faster than ever loaves and fishes grew before. And so Jesus kept on breaking up the bread and fish into pieces, and the bread and fish kept on increasing till all those five thousand hungry people had eaten just as much as they could eat. Then there were great piles of food lying all about. And Jesus said unto the disciples, 'Gather up the fragments . . . that nothing be lost. Therefore, they gathered them together, and filled twelve baskets with the fragments.' How very wonderful this was! Why, I suppose that one of those twelve baskets would have held all the loaves and fishes put together, before they began to eat of them. And yet, after five thousand people had eaten, there was twelve times more food left than there was before they began. This was surprising indeed! And how strange it was, that, in the midst of such abundance, Jesus should have been so particular in taking care of what was left! Why, we should have thought that if He could get it so easily, He wouldn't have taken any notice of the pieces left. But He did. If every piece of bread or fish had been a lump of gold, He couldn't have been more careful of them. This is very singular. What did Jesus do it for? He did it to teach us this important lesson—*never to waste anything.* When God made the great ocean, we are told that 'He *measured* the waters in the hollow of His hand,' so as to have neither too little nor too much, but just the quantity He wanted. When He made the mountains and hills, 'He *weighed* the mountains in scales, and the hills in a balance,' so as to have them just as large and as heavy as He desired them to be. God never wastes anything in the works that He performs. Suppose you set a pan of water out in the air where the sun can shine upon it in summer time. Now watch it. The sun makes the water warm; then you see a sort of steam rising up from the surface of the water. The sun is turning the water into vapour. It keeps on doing this. The water in the pan becomes less and less, till at last it is all gone. Perhaps you think that water is wasted, but it isn't. It has only changed its form. It has all turned to vapour. The vapour floats away in the clouds, and helps to make rain, and presently every drop of it will come down to earth again in the shape of rain. Not a single drop of all the water you had in your pan will be lost. There is no waste in anything that God does. And when Jesus, after performing this wonderful miracle, said, 'Gather up the fragments . . . that nothing be lost,' he intended to teach us not to be wasters of anything. Our sermon this afternoon will be *about gathering up the fragments.* Jesus spoke these words to the disciples about gathering up the fragments of bread and fish of which the people had been eating. But there are other kinds of fragments to be gathered. I wish now to speak of *four* different sorts of fragments which it is very important for us to learn how to gather.

In the first place, there are fragments of TIME *that we should gather up.*

Time is the most precious of all things. It is more valuable than gold or silver. When Elizabeth, the celebrated queen of England, was on her death-bed, she exclaimed, 'My kingdom for an hour of time!' But all the wealth and honours of her kingdom could not purchase for her the time she wanted. Queen Elizabeth had not wasted her time. Few persons had ever been more diligent in improving time than she had been. She was very fond of study. She used to rise early and spend every moment she could spare in reading and studying. She understood Greek and Latin perfectly. She could speak and write in five different languages; and one of the most learned men of her reign said, 'that she knew as much as any man then living.' I suppose that what the dying queen wanted time so much for, was to get ready for heaven. She had been very diligent in improving her time so far as reading and study was concerned, and in attending to the affairs of her kingdom, for she was one of the best monarchs that England ever had, but while doing this she had not taken care of her soul as she ought to have done. And when she came to die, she wanted more time to repent of her sins, and pray to God for His pardoning mercy. The right way to improve time is to take care of our souls *first;* to be sure and have them safe, by repenting and believing in Jesus, and then to gather up the fragments of time for other purposes.

A gentleman was once visiting the United States Mint. One room that he went into was called the gold room. Here the gold used in that establishment for making money was taken out and prepared for being melted. He noticed that the floor of this room was covered all over by a sort of grating, made of strips of wood, with openings between them. He asked what it was for. He was told, that it was intended to prevent any of the visitors from carrying away with the dust of their feet any of the very fine particles of gold which would fly off while they were filing the rough edges of the bars of gold. Every now and then they would take up this wooden grating from the floor and carefully sweep up the dust which collected there. Thus they gathered up these little fragments of gold, and from the sweepings of the floor they saved thousands of dollars in a year.

But time is worth more than gold; and if we were only as careful in gathering up its fragments as we should be, it is surprising how much of it we should be able to save.

Nearly all the persons who have become great and distinguished in the world, have early formed the habit of gathering up the fragments of their time, and never letting them slip idly by. If you read the lives of such men as Demosthenes the famous orator, of Julius Cæsar, Sir Isaac Newton, Franklin, Washington, Napoleon, you will find that they all had learned and practised well the lesson we are considering. They were very industrious. They gathered up the fragments of their time. They were no idlers. They rose early in the morning. They were busy all the day long. They used up all the odds and ends of their time. And you will never be able to do much, either for yourselves or others, unless you learn to gather up these fragments.

Some years ago a lean, awkward-looking boy, dressed in coarse, patched clothes, came one morning to the house in which the president of one of our eastern colleges lived. He knocked at the door, and asked to see the president. The servant-girl looked at his poor, shabby clothes, and thinking that he looked more like a beggar than anything else, told him to go round to the kitchen. The boy did as he was told, and soon appeared at the back door.

'I suppose you want some breakfast,' said the servant-girl, 'and I can give you that without troubling the doctor.'

'Thank you,' said the boy, 'I have no objection to the piece of bread; but I want very much to see the president.'

'Indeed,' said the girl, looking at the boy's patched trousers, 'I suppose you want some old clothes. I think the doctor has none to spare. He gives away a great many.' And then, without minding the boy's request, she went about her work.

The boy ate the bread with a keen relish, for he was very hungry. When he had finished it, he said, 'Can I see the president now?'

'Well, he's in the library; if he must be disturbed, he must, but he does like to be alone sometimes,' said the girl in a peevish tone. She seemed to think it very foolish to admit such an ill-looking fellow into her master's presence; but, wiping her hands, she told him to follow her. Opening the door of the library, she said:

'Here, sir, is somebody who is dreadfully anxious to see you, and so I let him in.'

The president looked towards the boy, and said:

'Well, my lad, what is it you want?'

'Please, sir,' said the boy, making an awkward sort of a bow, 'I want to know if I can enter college?'

'I should think not,' said the learned doctor, supposing from the boy's appearance that he was an ignorant fellow, who didn't know what he was talking about. He then asked him some questions in the simple rules of arithmetic, which he answered correctly. He then passed on to fractions and decimals, and to algebra; but all his questions were readily answered.

'Very good,' said the president. 'Do you know anything of Latin, my man?' asked he, handing the boy a copy of Virgil.

'A little. sir,' said the boy; and taking the book, he opened it, and read off a dozen or twenty lines very fluently, and translated them into English with great ease.

'Indeed!' said the doctor, as he looked at the boy with great surprise.

'Have you read any Greek, young man?' he asked, as he handed a copy of Homer.

'A little, sir,' said the boy again. He then took the book, and read and translated the Greek as easily as he had done the Latin.

'Upon my word,' said he, 'that is well done.' And looking at the youth over his spectacles, he asked: 'Why, my boy, when did you pick up all this learning?'

Now mark the boy's answer: '*In my spare moments, sir.*'

Ah yes, this boy had learned to gather up the fragments of time. He was a poor boy, who had to work hard on a farm for his living, and yet, by improving his spare moments—the half hour or quarter he could save at dinner-time, and by making use of the long winter evenings, after the day's work was done—he had prepared himself to enter college. While others were letting their spare moments slip idly away; while they were lounging about doing nothing, or, worse than nothing, learning to smoke and drink and to play cards, he was gathering up the fragments of his time that nothing should be lost. And if we could follow that young man through the rest of his life, we should expect to find him *making his mark* wherever he went, and rising to a high station among the wise and good men of the land.

A celebrated lawyer in France wrote a large and valuable law-book by taking the time he used to have to wait every day for his dinner to be ready.

There was a lady in France whose name was Madame de Genlis. She was the teacher of the princess in the royal family. Her pupil would often keep her waiting twenty minutes or half an hour when she came to give her her lesson. This was too much to lose. So she always carried a pencil and some paper with her, and in the course of several years she wrote two or three interesting volumes by just gathering up those fragments of time while she was waiting for her pupil.

There is a gentleman, now occupying a prominent position in England, who learned Latin and Greek while he was carrying messages as an errand-boy in the streets of Manchester.

Almost everybody has heard of Elihu Burritt, 'the learned blacksmith.' He is sometimes called 'the Buckeye blacksmith,' because he comes from Ohio, the Buckeye State. He has gone all over our country lecturing on different subjects. He was brought up as a blacksmith. And yet, while blowing the bellows, and wielding the hammer, he has contrived, by gathering the fragments of time, to learn *forty* different languages! How wonderful this is! And what he has done others may do, if they will but follow his example. Sometimes we hear business men say, 'Time is money.' But it is more than this. It can do for us what money never can. If rightly improved, it will make us learned and wise and good.

TIME AND KNOWLEDGE.

My dear young friends, let me entreat you to set a high value on your '*odd moments.*' Don't waste them. Begin now, while you are young, to make a good use of them. They are more precious than gold dust or diamond dust. Turn them all to good account. One of the Roman emperors used always to look back at night and see if his time had been well spent. If it had not, he would exclaim, 'I have lost a day.' Do not lose your hours or days in idleness, when by reading, or study, or labour, they can be made so profitable. Form the habit now of having all your hours usefully employed. It will be better for you than thousands of gold and silver.

Gather up the *fragments of time.*

But, secondly, *gather up the fragments of* KNOWLEDGE.

Knowledge is very useful. Almost everything that we learn will be of use to us some time or other. There is, in most houses, a little room called the store-room, or lumber-room. It is the place in which things are put that are not wanted at present. A strange collection of things you see when you go into that room. On the wall, at one side, hangs the tool board. Under this board stands the nail box. Near the nail box is another box which contains a great variety of things. There are keys, and old locks, and bolts, hinges and screws, hooks and staples, pieces of iron and brass. In one corner of the room are a number of old wooden boxes. On one of the shelves is a lot of empty bottles. Next to the bottles is a basket containing corks and pieces of leather. Behind the door are some boards and pieces of wood of different sizes. In one corner are some old shoes. In another is a broken table, and the remains of two or three old chairs. A wonderful variety of things may be found in that store-room. It is not very attractive to look at, but it is very useful. When anything gets out of order about the house, and some lock, or bolt, or hinge wants repairing; when a piece of board is needed in the kitchen, or a spike or a hook in the yard,—then the store-room is the place to go to. Whatever it is you want, you are almost sure to find it there. It is very important to have a store-room in a house. Yes, and it is very important to keep that room filled with all sorts of things. Whatever you put in there will come into use some time or other. Some of the things there may remain for years before you want them, but at last they will be just the things you want.

Now your mind may be compared to a house, and your memory is the store-room. Whatever you read or learn, or, in other words, all the knowledge you get, is stowed away in your memory just like the things you put by in your store-room. Every possible thing that you learn will be of use some time or other. Read all the good and useful books you can: get all the knowledge in your power, no matter what it's about, for some time in your life you will find it of service to you. You will have a full store-room with you wherever you go; and perhaps, when you least expect it, something that you learned years before will turn out to be the greatest help and comfort to you. Let me show you how this sometimes happens.

There is John Williams, the good missionary to the islands of the Pacific,—'the Martyr Missionary of Erromanga.' When he was a boy in England, he was engaged as a clerk in an ironmonger's shop. His duty was to attend in the shop to sell goods and receive orders. Back of the shop, and connected with it, was a large blacksmith's shop, where a number of men were employed in manufacturing different articles that were made of iron. Mr. Williams was not expected to work in this shop. But he was determined to learn everything about the business that he could. He had resolved to gather up all the fragments of knowledge in his power. And so, whenever he had half an hour or so to spare, at dinner time, or at the close of the day, he would go into the smiths' shop and get the men to show him how they did their work, and made the different articles of their trade. He kept on doing this till he had learned all about the business, and got to be one of the best workmen in the place; so that when any work to be done required particular skill and care, Mr. Williams was sure to be called upon to do it. Thus he gathered up the fragments there.

Now look at him again. He is on shipboard, going out to his labours in the South Seas. Here he tries to learn all he can from the sailors about the way in which a vessel is made, and rigged, and worked. Every day he is busy gathering up fragments of knowledge, and putting them away in the store-room of his memory. And see now what use he made of it all. Years have passed away. The people in the island of Raratonga, where he lives, have given up their idols and become Christians. The good missionary is anxious now to go to other islands, and tell the poor blind heathen there too about Jesus. But he has nothing to carry him there. What can he do? He thinks and prays over it awhile, and then resolves that he will try and build a vessel himself. What! in that far off island, with no timber and no proper tools, and nobody to help him, attempt to build a vessel! Yes, that is what he *tried* to do; and that is what he *did* do. He never rested till the little schooner called the *Messenger of Peace* was built and launched, and he was sailing away in her to tell of Jesus and His salvation to the heathen. You see now how useful those gathered fragments were to him! Unless the store-room of his memory had been filled with the knowledge of the way to work in iron which he had learned in England, and with the knowledge of how vessels were made and rigged, which he learned on shipboard, he never would have been able, when he became a missionary, to make a vessel for himself.

Every little bit and scrap of knowledge that you can pick up, you should put away in the store-room of memory. It will be sure to be of use to you some time or other. Let me tell you a story to prove this.

You know that the church of St. Peter's at Rome is one of the most splendid buildings in the world. There is a large open court in front of it which is filled with beautiful monuments and statuary. One of these is a beautiful obelisk made of Egyptian marble. An obelisk is a column of marble, or other stone, made out of one block, and gradually tapering off from one end to the other, so that the base on which it stands is broader than the top. The square tapering columns of marble that you see on tombstones are obelisks. But the one I am speaking of in front of St. Peter's at Rome is supposed to be the largest in the world. It is seventy-two feet high, twelve feet square at the base, and eight feet square at the top. It is said to be three thousand years old. It was found among the ruins of an old building in Rome, called the Circus of Nero. There it had lain buried for ages. But one of the popes determined to have it dug out, and cleaned, and set up among the other beautiful monuments in front of St. Peter's. He ordered this to be done. It was a very difficult job to move it. The obelisk was supposed to weigh about four hundred and seventy tons. Finally it was removed to the place appointed for it. There a pedestal, of solid stone, thirty feet high, was built for it to stand on. But to get that heavy mass on the top of the pedestal was no easy matter. The pope appointed a skilful architect to attend to it. He made all the necessary preparations. He got all the machinery ready, with the windlasses, blocks, ropes, tackling, and so forth. Then the pope fixed a day for setting up the obelisk. It was a grand holiday in Rome. All the people turned out to witness the sight. The pope's soldiers were there to keep the peace. The better to preserve order, the pope issued a proclamation, that, while the work was going on, no one, except those employed in the work, should speak a loud word, on pain of being put in prison. At last the arrangements are all made, and the order is given to hoist. The wheels go round—the ropes move—the blocks creak—and the obelisk begins to rise. The people watch it with great excitement, but in breathless silence. Higher and higher it goes. Everything seems to work well; and still it rises till it is within five or six inches of the place appointed for it, when suddenly it stops. What is the matter? The ropes have stretched so much that the blocks have come together too soon. They can't get it any higher. There it hangs dangling in the air. The people are disappointed. The architect is dreadfully excited. He is just on the point of ordering it to be lowered to the ground again, when an English sailor in the crowd, who had been watching the operation, sang out at the top of his voice, 'Wet the ropes—wet the ropes!' He had learned at sea that when new ropes are wet they always shrink and become shorter. This scrap of knowledge was very useful now. The architect saw that this would do it. The ropes were wet. They shrunk at once more than was needed, and the obelisk was landed in the place intended for it. The pope's soldiers took up the sailor and put him in prison. The next day he was brought up for trial, when the pope condemned him to receive a large sum of money for the fragment of knowledge which he had gathered up, and which was so very useful in that time of need. Jack took the punishment without a word of complaint.

I want now to give you one more illustration to show the importance of gathering up the fragments of scriptural knowledge, and that is all I shall say on this point of the subject.

There was a gentleman in New York who was an infidel. He never went to church. He had no Bible in the house. He did not believe that Jesus was a divine being, or that He died to save sinners. Yet, when this gentleman was a child he had a pious mother. She made him read the Bible. She filled the store-room of his memory with its precious promises. We shall see presently of what use these were to him. This gentleman was married. His wife was not a Christian. They had one child, a bright, intelligent little boy. The nurse of this child was a pious woman. She used often to talk to him about Jesus. She taught him the beautiful hymn—

> 'There is a happy land,
> Far, far away,' etc.

His parents, though they were not Christians, taught him to say his prayers at night, and often he would ask them questions about God and ' the happy land,' which they found it very hard to answer.

One evening the little fellow was lying on the bed partly undressed; his father and mother were seated by the fire. Tommy, as he was called, had not been a good boy that day. His mother had been telling his father what he had done, and how she had to punish him for it. All was quiet for a while, when suddenly the child broke out in a loud sobbing and crying which surprised his parents. His father went to him and asked what was the matter.

'I don't want it, father; I don't want it there,' said he.

'What is it, my child, what is it?' he asked.

'Why, father, I don't want the angels to write down in God's book all the bad things I have done to-day. I don't want it there. I wish it could be wiped out.' Then he cried again bitterly, and his father was almost ready to cry with him. What could he do? I said his father was an infidel. But now he put aside his infidelity. He remembered the truths of the Bible which his mother had taught him when *he* was a child. He turned to them now, and tried to comfort his distressed child with them.

'Don't cry, my dear child,' he said, 'you can have it all wiped out in a minute if you want.'

'How, father, how?' asked Tommy eagerly.

'Why, get down on your knees, and ask God for Christ's sake to wipe it out, and He will do it.'

TIME AND KNOWLEDGE. 131

He didn't have to speak twice. In an instant Tommy jumped out of bed, and kneeled down by the bedside. He put up his little hands and was just about beginning, when he looked up and said—

'O father, won't you come and help me?'

This was a hard thing to ask. His father had never really prayed in his life. But he saw the great distress of his child, and how could he refuse? So the proud infidel man got down on his knees by the side of his dear boy, and asked God to wipe away his sins. Then they got up, and Tommy went into bed again. In a few moments he looked up and said—

'Father, are you *sure* it's all wiped out?'

What a question was this to ask an infidel! But he felt that he must give up his infidelity, as he answered —'Why, yes, the Bible says, if you ask God from your heart for Christ's sake to do it, and if you are really sorry for what you have done, it shall be all blotted out.'

A sweet smile passed over the face of the child as he laid his little head upon the pillow. But presently he sat up again in bed and said, 'Father, what did the angel wipe it out with?—with a sponge?'

This was another question that almost staggered his father. He had been in the habit of saying that it was not necessary for Christ to shed His blood that men might be pardoned. But now he felt in a moment that it *was* necessary. He could not answer his child's question unless this was true. So he said—

'No, my child, not with a sponge, but with the blood of Christ. The Bible says, "The blood of Jesus Christ cleanseth from all sin."'

Then Tommy was satisfied, and soon fell asleep. From that hour his father gave up his infidelity, and became a Christian. Here you see how useful to him were those gathered fragments of Bible knowledge which he had stowed away in his memory.

Now, my dear young friends, remember about these

two kinds of fragments you are to gather. Begin at once to gather up the fragments of time and the fragments of knowledge. Form the habit now while you are young, and it will be of more value to you than you can tell.

IX.

Gathering the Fragments: Money and Usefulness.

'Gather up the fragments . . . that nothing be lost.'—JOHN vi. 12.

IN our last sermon on this text we spoke about two kinds of fragments that ought to be gathered up. These were *fragments of* TIME *and fragments of* KNOWLEDGE.

The third kind of fragments to be gathered is the *fragments of* MONEY.

There are two reasons why we should gather up the fragments of money. *We ought to do it for our own good, and we ought to do it for the good of others.*

We should gather up the fragments of money for our own benefit. Pounds are made up of pence; and Benjamin Franklin used to say, 'If we take care of the *pence* the pounds will take care of themselves.'

A boy worked hard all day for a shilling. With that shilling he bought some apples. He went along the streets and sold the apples for four shillings. With the money he bought a sheep. The sheep brought him a lamb. For the fleece of the lamb he got four shillings. With this money he bought another sheep. The next spring he had two sheep, two lambs, and a yearling sheep. He sold the three fleeces for twelve shillings, and bought three more sheep. Now he had six sheep, and a fair prospect of doing well with them. He worked hard, and gathered up the fragments of money, so as to be able to get hay, and corn, and oats, and pasture for his sheep. He took the greatest care of his lambs and sheep, and soon he had a good-sized flock. Their wool enabled him to buy a pasture for them. By the time he was twenty-one years old he had a good start in business, and after a few years he became a wealthy farmer. Sometimes when he was showing persons about over his splendid, well-stocked farm, worth thousands of pounds, he used to say that he got it all for a *shilling*. Then he would tell them of the time when he worked hard all day for a shilling, and began to trade with that. That shilling was the foundation of his fortune. He learned to gather up the fragments of money for his own benefit.

There is a young man in Massachusetts now who is doing a flourishing business. He is a fine, intelligent man. Everybody who knows him respects and loves him. He began his life in a very similar way to the boy just spoken of; only, instead of buying a sheep with the first money he had earned and saved, he bought a book with it. His parents were very poor. They taught him to be careful of his pennies, to gather up the fragments of money. He did not get much, but he took good care of what he did get. He saved up his pennies till he had fifty of them—the first silver he ever had. He laid out this money in buying a Bible—the Book of books. When he got this Bible he resolved to read it daily, and pray God for grace to help him to live according to its teachings. Thus in taking his start in life, he planted himself on the Bible. While doing this he still went on gathering up the fragments. He was careful of the little money he received. As fast as he got money enough to do so, he bought other useful and instructive books. He read them over, in his leisure hours, with the greatest care and interest. He grew up to be a model young man. And now he is very rich, and carrying on a large business, and is one of the first men in the town in which he lives. But if he had spent the first money he ever owned in drinking, or gambling, or going to the theatre, instead of buying a Bible, he might have been a miserable drunkard, without wealth, or character, or usefulness. He gathered the fragments of money for his own benefit.

In looking over my scrap-book the other day to find something to illustrate this point, I met with an anecdote headed, 'A Gold Watch in a Rag-Bag.' On reading it over, I found it was just the thing for this part of the sermon, and so I must put it in here.

A lady who lived near Bridgeport, in Connecticut, was in the habit of putting out shirts to make, to a number of women, for a large clothing establishment in the neighbourhood. In cutting these out there were a great many pieces left—little odds and ends too small to be of use. The first thought was to toss them into the fire. But, 'no,' she said to herself, ' I'll "gather up the fragments" and save them. Perhaps I may get enough by and by to exchange them with the tinman for something or other that may be useful in the kitchen.' So she gathered them up and put them away, and in a few weeks there was quite a pile of them.

One day a neighbour came in, and on hearing what she was going to do with her scraps, he advised her to send them to a paper-mill which was not far off. 'They will give you twopence a pound for them,' said he, 'and that is better than to exchange them with the tinman.'

She asked her husband's advice. To him a few rags seemed like a matter of no consequence.

'Do just as you like,' said he laughingly. '*You* may have all the money you can make out of the rags.'

She took him at his word, and in two or three months some half-dozen barrels of rags were sent to the paper-mill. To her surprise, she received in return for these a nice new sovereign. When this was handed to her, the first thought that came into her mind was to go out and buy some ornamental thing for the house. But after thinking over it a little while, she came to a different conclusion. She resolved still to 'gather up the fragments.'

She said to herself, 'No, I won't spend it. All my rag money shall go into the savings bank.'

And into the savings bank it went. Time rolled on. More rags were saved and sold. The money kept steadily increasing.

One day a tempting opportunity presented itself of purchasing a fine gold watch. The price of the watch was eight pounds.

'I will not ask my husband to take that much money out of his business,' said the lady to herself. 'Now is the time to make use of my rag money.'

The watch was purchased—literally, with rags. It was truly *a gold watch gotten out from a rag-bag!*

But this was not the end of it. The money in the savings bank, which grew out of a bundle of rags, went on increasing for a number of years after the gold watch had been bought, and now it amounts to *over five hundred pounds!* Only think of it!

'I am surprised to think how it has increased,' said the lady one day to some of her friends. 'A few cuttings and scraps laid aside, when I cut out shirts— a few dollars carried to the bank when I went into town—a little interest added on from time to time—a few fragments gathered up with care, this was all; and yet it has grown into this snug little fortune.'

Certainly this lady gathered up the fragments of money for her own benefit.

But then we ought to gather them up too *for the good of others.*

A little boy once attended a missionary meeting, and was very much interested in the speeches that were made. When he got home he tried to think of something that he could do to help on the good cause. But he could think of nothing that was of any importance. He was very young, and he felt that he would have to live many years before he could expect to speak about the work, as he had heard the gentlemen do at that meeting. He was very poor, and all he had seemed worth nothing as he thought of the gold and silver which others had to give. All the money he had in the world consisted of a solitary farthing which somebody had given him. It was a new, bright, beautiful little coin, but still it was only a farthing—and what good could that do? At last he resolved to send it to the minister whose speech had interested him most at the missionary meeting. The minister had come from London, and the little boy thought he had better put the farthing in a letter, and send it to him by post. So he folded it up nicely in a piece of paper, and wrote a letter with it in this style:

'DEAR SIR,—I am but a very little boy, and am very poor. My father and mother can give me nothing to send to the Missionary Society; I have only a farthing of my own. Still I want to give something, so I send this farthing to you. 'G. B. S.'

Away went the letter with its farthing, and great was the delight of the gentleman on getting it. He was just about setting out on a visit to Scotland, to hold missionary meetings in different places, so he took the farthing and the letter with him. Wherever he held a meeting he showed the farthing and read the letter. Everybody was pleased. The young people especially were stirred up by it to raise some money, and before the gentleman returned to London the little boy's solitary farthing had gained above forty pounds. Here you see how that little boy's gathered fragment—a single farthing —was made to promote the *good of others*.

Now let me tell you of another case in which the same thing was done by a little boy in a different way.

'Mother, I've got a penny, may I go and spend it?' asked little Freddy one day as he twirled the new, bright coin in his fingers.

'What do you wish to get with it, my son?' asked his mother.

'Oh, I don't know,' said he, casting his eyes down. 'A stick of candy, or gum, or something.'

'You know, Freddy,' said his mother, 'I don't like you to eat candy or chew gum, and there is nothing else you can get for a penny that you will care for at all five minutes after you get it. I do wish, my son, that your pennies did not trouble you so much.'

'Trouble me, mother! Why, what do you mean?'

'I mean just what I say, dear; for as soon as you get one you want to spend it. And as you can't do so without displeasing me, or doing yourself harm, I think they are more trouble than pleasure to you.'

'Oh dear!' said Freddy, throwing himself on the floor, and drawing a long sigh, 'I don't know *what* to do; I'm sure I wish I *could* spend my money somehow.'

'Freddy,' said his mother, 'did you ever think how much good your pennies might do, if you would only save them till you got a good many of them together, and then give them to some poor person, or buy a nice book to give to some poor child who has no books or schools as you have?'

'Why, mother, I never thought of that,' said Freddy, brightening up. 'I'll try to save my pennies after this, and see what good I can do with them.'

Freddy ran into his own little room, and dropped his penny into a small box which stood on the table. After this he went on carefully gathering up the fragments. Whenever a penny was given to him he would add it to his treasure in the box. He told his mother, one day, that the pennies didn't trouble him any more since he had found out what to do with them. He liked to get money and save it that he might do good with it.

One day, about two or three months after this, Freddy came home from school in a great hurry. He ran into the house, and without stopping to speak to any one, rushed into his own room, seized his money-box, emptied it, and was off again before his mother had time to notice what he was doing. In about half an hour he came back again, looking very bright and happy.

'Why, Freddy,' said his mother, 'what does all this mean? Why did you run into the house and fly out again without stopping to speak to any one?'

'O mother, please excuse me. I was in such a hurry I forgot all about it. I wanted my pennies to buy a new slate for little Sally Brown. She fell down and broke hers just as she was coming out of the schoolroom. You know the people she lives with don't love her, and would have whipped her if she had carried home the broken one. So I told her not to cry, but walk slowly on, and I would get her a new one in a few minutes. I was in such a dreadful hurry because her mistress would scold her if she wasn't home at the usual time. I am *so* glad, mother, that I followed your advice and saved my pennies. I'm sure it was nicer to help poor Sally in her trouble than to have had *all the candy in town to eat.*'

Freddy remembered his mother's good advice afterwards. He kept on gathering up the fragments, and so often had it in his power to do good to others in a way that made him feel truly happy. We should 'gather up the fragments' of money *for our own good and for the good of others.*

But there is still another kind of fragments that we should gather up; it is the fourth and last kind. I refer to the FRAGMENTS OF USEFULNESS. I mean, by this, that we should be careful to improve all the opportunities for usefulness that come in our way. There are a great many different ways in which we may be useful, if we only try to improve them, by gathering up these fragments as we find them lying in our path.

We may be useful by our example, and we should improve every opportunity of doing good in this way. I was reading lately of a little boy who 'gathered up the fragments' about him in this way, and was the means of doing good. The little fellow was only about ten or eleven years old. He was the son of a clergyman. His father had got a situation for him on board one of those ships where boys are put in order to be trained and educated for officers in the navy. This little boy's father and mother, being good Christians, had taught him carefully to pray to God every morning and evening, and had told him to be sure and do this wherever he might go.

When the little fellow went on board the great ship, he found himself surrounded by a large company of other boys. Some of them were older and some younger than himself. They were cadets and midshipmen, who were to be his companions, and who were very fond of fun and play, as boys generally are. He got along with them very well till the time came to go to bed in the evening. A bell was rung as a signal for the boys to go to their berths, as the beds are called on shipboard. The boys were laughing and talking and playing tricks of various kinds while getting undressed. George, as our little friend was named, looked round to see if none of them kneeled down to pray before going to bed, but not one of them did so. He remembered what he had been taught at home; he thought how God had taken care of him all the day, how only He could preserve him through the night, and he felt that he could not go to bed without prayer. Then the temptation occurred to him, 'But can't I pray as heartily when lying in my bed, as if I should kneel down to pray? and then the boys won't laugh at me.' But then the thought occurred, that it would please his mother better if he should kneel down to pray, and a better thought still came into his mind, that it would please God. This decided him. He knelt down to pray. Immediately all the thoughtless boys around began to laugh at him. One called him a Methodist; another said he was the parson. One threw a book at him, another threw a pillow at him. But the little fellow still knelt on till he had finished his prayer. The next night he was interrupted in the same way, and so it continued night after night. And yet the brave little fellow would kneel down and offer his prayers to God. He never complained of the conduct of the boys. But some one else about the ship found out how the boys were behaving in their cabin at night, and went and told the captain.

Now it happened that the captain was a good, pious man, and he resolved to put a stop to the bad conduct of the boys. The next day he had all the boys called up before him on the deck of the ship. Then he called George up to him and said:

'Well, my little fellow, have you any complaint to make of the conduct of these boys?'

'No, sir,' said George.

'Now, boys,' said the captain, 'George will tell no tales and make no complaints; but I have heard how you have been teasing and persecuting him at night, because he had the courage to kneel down and pray to that God who takes care of him. I have only this to say; if any of you shall dare to do this again, I'll have you tied up on deck, and try how you like the taste of a rope's end on your back. Now go to your duties.'

All the boys felt guilty. They would hardly speak to George during the rest of the day. But when evening came again, George knelt down as usual to pray. There was no laughing or talking. They were all as still as mice. George had not been kneeling long before he felt something at his side coming close up to him. He looked round to see what it was, and found one of the little boys who was nestling close up to him, that he too might say his prayers in peace and quietness. Presently another came, and then another, till at last quite a number were found kneeling round him. These boys had all been taught to pray at home; but when they were surrounded by rude, mocking boys, they had not courage enough to do what was right, by acknowledging their dependence on God, before their companions. But the influence of George's example, when he quietly and bravely took his stand, determined to do right himself whatever others did, encouraged them to do so too. From that time prayer was never neglected on board that ship, while even those who did not pray themselves were afraid or ashamed to laugh or mock at those who did. In this way little George was very useful to his young companions by the example which he set them. We should 'gather up the fragments' of usefulness that lie around us, by setting a good example.

We may be useful by our WORDS, as well as by our example; and we should 'gather up the fragments,' by improving every opportunity that offers of doing good in this way.

'Sir,' said an old man one day to a minister, 'would you like to know how I, an old grey-headed sinner, was led to become a Christian?'

'Yes, sir,' replied the minister; 'I should like very well to hear it.'

'Well, sir, I was walking along the street one day, and met a little boy. The little fellow stepped up to me, and made a polite bow and said, in a kind, gentle way, " Please, sir, will you take a tract, and please, sir, will you read it?"

'Now, I had always hated tracts; and when anybody offered them to me, I used to get angry, and swear dreadfully at them. But that " please, sir," overcame me. I could not swear at that gentlemanly little fellow, with his kind-spoken " Please, sir :" no, no. So I took the tract, and thanked the little boy for it. I promised him I'd read it; and I did read it, and the reading of it was a great blessing to me. It led me to see that I was a sinner. It showed me that Jesus Christ is the only Saviour. It was the means of making me a Christian. That " please, sir," was the key that unlocked my hard old heart.' That little boy was gathering up the fragments of usefulness. He was trying to do good by his words.

Sometimes there is wonderful power in a few simple words to do good, even though they are spoken by a child.

Some years ago there was a man in Scotland whose name was James Stirling. He had been an honest, industrious man, and lived happy with his family. But in an evil hour he learned to love strong drink. He became a drunkard. Then poverty and want and misery came into his little cottage. His poor wife was a pious woman. She struggled hard, working day and night, to support her family. Through years of grief and sorrow she laboured on, still hoping and praying that God would turn her husband from his evil ways, and make him a sober man again. At last her prayer was heard. Her husband gave up drinking. He signed the temperance pledge. Then their home was happy again. James Stirling became a great temperance man, and was the means of saving hundreds of his countrymen from going down to a drunkard's grave. But how was this change brought about? Let me tell you.

Stirling's faithful wife had always been in the habit of having family prayers with her children when her husband was absent. One night she sat down with a heavy heart, and her eyes full of tears, to read the Bible to her children, and to pray with them. What follows I must tell you in James Stirling's own language:

'I had been out all day at the tavern, and at night, when I came home, my wife as usual was reading a chapter to the children. I entered the door as she was so engaged, slipping in like a condemned criminal. The portion of Scripture read was the twenty-fifth of Matthew, in which these words occur: "When the Son of Man shall come in His glory, and all the holy angels with Him, then shall He sit upon the throne of His glory; and before Him shall be gathered all nations; and He shall separate them one from another, as a shepherd divideth the sheep from the goats; and He shall set the sheep on His right hand, but the goats on His left."

Our youngest boy, then about four years old, was lying with his head on his mother's lap; and just when she read those awful words, he looked up earnestly into her face and asked, "*Mother, will father be a goat then?*"

'This was more than I could stand. The earnest, innocent look of the poor child, the astonishment of the poor mother, and above all, the question itself, went right to my heart. I never slept a wink all that night. I felt that I would rather die than go on living as I had been living. I resolved that night, that with the help of God, all the men on earth should never tempt me to drink intoxicating liquor again.'

And the resolution that James Stirling made that night he kept for thirty years, when he died beloved and honoured by all who knew him. Only think how much good was done by the short, simple question of that little child!

When we try to 'gather up the fragments' of usefulness, we cannot tell how much good may spring from the least thing we do. A minister was making an address at a meeting one day. He was urging all the people to try and make themselves useful. Among the persons present, he saw a plain working-man, standing with a little girl in his arms. The speaker was urging the importance of our trying to do good in every way in our power. 'Everybody has some influence, even to that child,' said he, pointing to the little girl in her father's arms. 'That's true!' cried the man, forgetting, for a moment, where he was. After the meeting was over, he stepped up to the minister, and said: 'I beg your pardon, sir. I didn't intend to interrupt you in your address, but I couldn't help speaking. Not long ago, sir, I was a drunkard; but as I didn't like to go to the tavern alone, I used to carry this dear child with me. As I came near the house one night, hearing a great noise inside, she said, "Don't go, father." "Hold your tongue, child," I said. "Oh, please, father, don't go!" "Hold your tongue," I said again, shaking her rudely. She said no more. But presently I felt the big, warm tears falling on my cheek. I couldn't go a step farther, sir. I turned round and went home. I have never been to the tavern since. By the help of God, I never mean to go again. I am a happy man now, sir; and my family are all happy. This dear child has done it all; and when you said, even she has influence, I couldn't help saying, " That's true." All have influence.'

Now let us see, how many kinds of fragments have we spoken of altogether? Four. Yes. What are they? *Fragments of time; fragments of knowledge; fragments of money;* and *fragments of usefulness.*

Well, let us all resolve to be earnest and diligent in trying to gather up these different fragments. The least, and the youngest of us, may find enough to do in this way. Don't say, 'Oh, I'm too little; I can't do anything!' Nobody is too little to 'gather up fragments.' Fragments are little things, and little people are just the ones to gather them. If you pick up a tiny pebble, not bigger than the end of your little finger, and throw it into a pond, you know how it will make a circular ripple on its smooth surface, that will go on getting wider and wider, till at last it reaches the shore. And just so, when we try to do good in any of the ways we have been speaking of, the fragment that we gather of time, or knowledge, or money, or usefulness, like the ripple on the pond, may spread itself out for good to all who are round about us. If we ever expect to be good or great, we must begin by being good and great in little things. The great Academy of Music in New York was built by just laying one brick upon another. The great Pyramids in Egypt, which are like young mountains, were made by laying one stone upon another. Oh, gather up the fragments, then. Begin to do good in a small way, and others will soon open before you.

I will close my sermon by repeating some sweet, simple lines which I met with the other day. They are just the thing for those who want to begin to be fragment gatherers. They are entitled:

LITTLE DEEDS.

'Not mighty deeds make up the sum
   Of happiness below,
But little acts of kindliness,
   Which any child may show.

'A merry sound, to cheer the babe,
   And tell a friend is near;
A word of ready sympathy,
   To dry the childish tear;

'A glass of water, kindly brought;
   An offered easy chair;
A turning of the window blind,
   That all may feel the air;

'An early flower, unasked, bestowed;
   A light and cautious tread;
A voice to gentlest whisper hushed,
   To spare the aching head:

'Oh, deeds like these, though little things,
   Yet purest love disclose,
As fragrant perfume on the air
   Reveals the hidden rose.

'Our heavenly Father loves to see
   These precious fruits of love;
And if we only serve Him here,
   We'll dwell with Him above.'

X.

The Best Helper.

'*I will help thee.*—Isaiah xli. 10.

TWO persons are spoken of here: *I* and *thee*. 'I,' the person speaking, is Jesus, our God and Saviour; and 'thee,' the person spoken to, means everybody who needs His help and seeks it. This is one of the promises of Christ. He says, they are *all* 'exceeding great and precious;' and this promise is one of the *most* precious in the Bible.

It is precious, because it belongs to so many people. Suppose it had said, 'I will help the Queen of England,' it would then only belong to *one* person in this country. Suppose the promise had been, 'I will help the ministers of the gospel, or the Sunday-school teachers,—the rich or the poor,—the young or the old;'—then it would refer only to a small number of persons. But it does not mention any particular class of people. It says, 'I will help *thee*.' This means you and me, and everybody who needs it, and comes to Jesus for it.

In this passage, Jesus is presented to our notice as a *helper*. We may have many helpers, but Jesus is the best.

There are *four* reasons why Jesus is the Best Helper! He is so, in the first place, because He is ALWAYS NEAR TO HELP.

It is of no use to have a helper, unless he is always

near when we need him. If we were hungry, it would not help us to know that a hundred miles off there was a nice loaf of bread. If we were travelling in the desert of Arabia, where it is very hot and sandy, and we were parched, and almost dead with thirst, would it help us any to remember that in America there were many cool and sparkling springs of water? We might own a hundred such springs in this country, but they could do us no good then,—we want help near us when we need it.

You have all heard of Sir John Franklin and his crew. Some years ago they went off towards the North Pole, and they have never been heard of since. I suppose they got through the first winter pretty comfortably, but the second was very severe; and when it came, it found them entangled in the ice, without wood to make fires and keep out the cold, and without food to eat. What was to be done? There were many desiring to help them, but they were far off in England. There was the wife of Sir John Franklin, a rich lady; she would have parted with all she had in the world to bring back her husband. There, too, was Queen Victoria; she would have taken the brightest jewel from her crown, if that would have relieved the sufferings of the lost crew. There were the officers of the British navy; they all would have gone to their relief; the American navy, too, would gladly have helped them. And there was that good man in New York, Mr. Grinnell, who would have given thousands of pounds to find them; and that noble-hearted American, Dr. Kane, who went in search of them,—but it was all in vain. They had plenty of helpers, but they were not near enough to help them.

And here, perhaps, some one may be ready to ask, why God, who was near these perishing men, did not send them help. God is always near when people are in trouble. He always *could* help them if He saw it best. But sometimes He sees good reasons for not helping those who are in need.

THE BEST HELPER.

For instance, there are the wicked men nailing Jesus to the cross. He is God's own dear Son. God loves Him as no other father ever loved a son. God is near. He sees all His sufferings. The angels of heaven see it. Multitudes of them would fly in an instant to His relief, if God would let them. But no! He suffers not one of them to move. God would not send help to His only begotten Son when the men were putting Him to death.

And *why* was this? Ah! there was reason enough for it. If Jesus had not died, none of us would have been saved. Was not *that* a good reason? And just so in every case where God does not help people, there is always a good reason for it, though we cannot always tell what the reason is.

There was once a poor woman, the widow of a clergyman, who trusted in God and served Him. In times of trouble she often used to say to her children and friends, 'Do not fear; *God lives,* and He will take care of us.' But after her husband's death, she was left to struggle with sickness and poverty. Her trials were very great. She tried to bear up under them with the patience and cheerfulness of a Christian, and, generally, she was successful. But on one occasion, when she was particularly afflicted, her faith seemed to fail for a little while, and giving way to her feelings of grief and sadness, she burst into tears.

Her little son, who was just able to talk, saw her weeping, and putting his hand in hers, and looking into her face very sadly, he said, 'Mother, is God dead now?' Taking him in her arms, she said, 'No, my son, God is not dead. I thank you for asking that question. He always lives. He is an ever present help in every time of need. He will help us.' She wiped away her tears, and went cheerfully to her duties. She sought and found help from Jesus.

Thus, my dear children, Jesus is the *Best Helper,* because *He is always near.*

The second reason why He is the Best Helper is, because HE IS ALWAYS ABLE TO HELP.

Sometimes there are many helpers, and they are near at hand, but they are *not able to help*.

A wealthy gentleman has a darling child, a little girl, five or six years old. She is the joy of her parents' hearts, the light of their dwelling. Like a sunbeam she gladdens all around her. But this dear child is taken sick; the doctor is sent for; he comes, he sees her; he looks at her flushed face, he feels her pulse, he examines her symptoms, and says she has the scarlet fever.

Her father and mother feel very anxious about their dear child. But as the fever increases, the doctor looks very sad, and says: 'I'm afraid I can't help her.' Her mother is almost distracted. They call in other physicians. These gather round the bed; they try different medicines; they do everything that can be thought of, but they cannot save her. The fever becomes higher and higher, and at last death takes the little sufferer away. Many helpers are there, but they are not able to save.

Some time ago a man was carried down the Niagara river among the rapids above the great Fall. He soon lost command of the boat. His oars were swept from his hand, and at last the boat was upset. He was seen for a while to struggle with the rapids, which bore him on toward the fearful gulf. In his swift course he passed by a clump of trees whose branches hung over into the stream from a little island. He caught one of the branches, and hung awhile in the midst of the foaming waves, and finally succeeded in getting upon the island. Soon the cry was heard,—'A man in the rapids! A man in the rapids!' People came in crowds to the banks of the river. They look upon the poor man with intense interest and pity. Many sympathizing hearts and willing hands are there; but they cannot reach the unfortunate man to help him.

At last they get a little boat, fasten a strong rope to it, place it in the rapids, and let out the rope. It goes gradually down toward the island on which the poor man stands, trembling on the brink of ruin. He watches eagerly the preparations his friends are making for his rescue. He sees the boat which they are letting down to him. He prepares to catch hold of it; he knows it is his only hope of safety. If he misses that, he is gone.

Ah! how intensely he watches the boat as it comes near him! How earnestly, too, the sympathizing people on the shore watch it, as the rough waters tumble it about. See! . . . it reaches him. He gathers all his strength,— he makes one plunge,—but, alas! he misses the boat! The foaming waters receive him, and 'Lost! lost!' is the heartrending cry from the multitudes on the shore, as he rushes over the fearful precipice.

Now, you see, hundreds of kind hearts and strong hands were there, willing and anxious to rescue that poor man, but they *were not able.* It is very different, however, with Jesus. He is *always near* and *always able* to help us.

We read a great deal in the Bible about those whom Jesus has helped. There we find how He helped Abel when he offered an acceptable sacrifice to God. He helped Noah to build the ark, which saved himself and his family. He helped Moses to lead the children of Israel out of Egypt. He helped David to slay the great giant, with nothing in his hand but a sling and a stone. He helped Daniel, when he was cast into the lions' den, and shut the lions' mouths, so that they did not hurt him. He helped Daniel's three friends when they were thrown into the burning fiery furnace, and enabled them to walk up and down in the midst of the flames without being scorched. He helped Paul to preach the gospel; and, in the days of cruel persecution, He helped the 'noble army of martyrs' to bear with patience the chain and the dungeon; yea, and even to sing for joy when the flames were kindling around them and the fire consuming their bodies.

And there, too, was Martin Luther, that brave soldier

of the cross, who carried on the work of the Reformation when the pope, and the cardinals, and the emperor, and all the kingdoms and powers of the earth were trying to put him down. Jesus helped him, and made him bold and courageous, so that he never feared or faltered in his course. And it was because of the help that Jesus gave him that he was able to go on successfully with his great work. The pope and the priests of Rome were full of fury against him, and tried with all their might to stop him, but they could not.

Rich men can help us with their money, wise men with their counsels, and Christians with their prayers; but Jesus can help us in everything. He can help you, my dear children, in studying your lessons, and in all your daily duties.

A gentleman once said to a little girl, 'Mary, do you have to learn very hard lessons?' 'Oh yes, sir,' she replied; 'but before I begin to study them I pray to God to help me, and that makes them easy'—and so it will make everything easy. Try it for yourselves. Jesus will help all who ask Him to resist temptation; He will help them to repent, and to believe in Him, and to forsake all their evil ways.

He can help kings and governors to rule, and subjects to obey. He can help ministers to preach, and people to hear. He can help parents and children, teachers and scholars. He is able and willing to help all who feel their need of help, and truly seek his aid. Paul said, 'I can do *all things* through Christ strengthening (or helping) me.' And you and I may say and do the same, if we look to Him for His help. Jesus then is the Best Helper, because *He is always able to help.*

The *third* reason why Jesus is the Best Helper is, *because* HE IS ALWAYS WILLING TO HELP.

He may not always be willing to help us just at the time, or in the way we desire,—that may not be best; but in His own time and way He is always willing to help.

THE BEST HELPER.

We read in the Bible about the rich man and Lazarus. The rich man was *able* to help, but he was not *willing*. The poor beggar sat at his gate every day. The rich man had an abundance of this world's goods, and could have given him comfortable clothing and plenty of food, but he would not give him anything. The helper, in this case, was near at hand, and able, but not willing.

There was once a ship that took fire at sea. Fire is a fearful thing to encounter anywhere, but it is never so fearful as at sea; for although in the very midst of water, there are no means of using it to put the fire out. There were about two hundred people on board this ship; and as the flames increased, and roared among the masts and rigging, they all crowded to one end of the vessel, screaming, and running to and fro in dreadful distress. As night came on, a vessel hove in sight. It came nearer and nearer, until it was close enough to hear the shrieks of the people calling for help, and to see them wringing their hands in despair. The sailors on board the approaching ship were ready to go to the assistance of those distressed people, waiting only for their captain's order—but no order was given. At last the mate said to him, 'Sir, had we not better lower the boat?' But all the answer he received from the inhuman captain was, 'Mind your own business, sir.' He had a rich cargo of goods to sell, and he was in great haste to reach the port for which he was bound. He saw the burning ship, and two hundred people threatened with an awful death; yet he steeled his heart against every feeling of pity, and would not allow the man at the helm to alter his course. He turned from his fellow-creatures, and left them to perish by water or by fire. This wretched man was near enough to help, and able enough to help; but, ah! he was *not willing*.

Now Jesus is always willing. He may not send the help just in the way we wish, but in one way or other He is sure to send it. He tells us in the Bible that He is more willing to help those who come to Him than parents are to give bread to their children. When you are hungry, and go to your father or mother for something to eat, you know how readily they give it to you; yet Jesus is more ready to help us than earthly parents are to feed their children.

When General Washington was fighting for his country, he called upon the name of the Lord, and the Lord heard and answered him. When the first Congress of the United States met in the Hall of Independence to frame the constitution and make the laws by which they were to be governed, they had a difficult task to perform. They met time after time, but could not agree about the constitution or the laws, and they were likely to break up in confusion. One day, that wise and good man, Benjamin Franklin, rose and said, in substance: 'My friends, we need some one stronger and wiser than we are to help us. I move that we have a minister of the gospel to pray for us.' The motion was seconded, and they secured a chaplain. He prayed to God to help them in their trouble. His prayer was heard. Jesus helped them. He gave the wisdom they needed to enable them to frame the constitution and laws under which we live, and by which our country enjoys so many blessings.

Two men were once associated together during their young days and through their college life; but leaving college, they were separated from each other. One resided in a large city, and was prospered by the hand 'that maketh rich.' He became wealthy, and ever sought to honour God in the use of the means bestowed upon him.

The other became a clergyman, and went as a missionary to the far West. On the Sabbath, he was engaged in breaking the Bread of Life to the hardy but poor settlers around him, and during the week he toiled for earthly food, to sustain a young family. Years had passed since the two friends had met; nor had news of one reached the other. They were ignorant of each other's circumstances—almost of their location.

One day, while the merchant was engaged in his business, the thought of his absent and almost forgotten friend came suddenly to his mind. During the day, at every interval from his busy cares, he found himself thinking about his old friend. He tried to find out what it was which had led him to think about him, but in vain. In the evening, when he returned home, the image of his early companion was still before his mind. That one so long almost forgotten should come so vividly to remembrance, he felt was singular. He mentioned the circumstance to his wife, and asked if she could account for it. She suggested that his friend might be in need of assistance, and at all events it would be well to write him, enclosing a sum of money; it might prove a great help to a poor missionary toiling in the West.

The letter was sent. Weeks rolled on, and an answer was received. In the humble home of the missionary fever had laid its hand upon every inmate. Mother and children all lay upon beds of sickness, unable to assist each other. The father, in the intervals of his attack, was nurse and provider for his sick family. Ill and feeble himself, yet he must ride many miles to a mill, carrying with him the Indian corn, to procure for his little ones the only food they had to keep them alive. At last even this supply was gone, and without money, or food, or the means of obtaining either, he betook himself to his knees, praying that the God 'who feedeth the ravens' would provide for his children. Trusting in a covenant-keeping Father, he arose from his prayer, cheered and comforted. Shortly after there came a knock at his door. He opened it, and received a letter. With a heart swelling with thankfulness, he read the warm and affectionate greeting from the friend of his boyhood.

Enclosed in it he found a sum sufficient for himself and his children for some months, and want was again driven from his dwelling. Ah! how welcome it was to him. It came just in the right time,—in his greatest need,—and he felt that Jesus was indeed willing to help His people in every time of trouble.

Yes! He is *near to help, able to help*, and *willing to help*.

There is only one other reason I will give you why Jesus is the Best Helper. Because HE is ALWAYS KIND IN HELPING.

Now there are some people who are willing and able to help others, and who do help them too, but it is done in a very rough manner.

Even ministers are sometimes harsh in their way of giving counsel or reproof.

There was once a minister who had a kind heart, and who was very anxious to do good, but he did it in a very rough way. He reproved people about trifling things with unnecessary severity. Upon one occasion, when several ministers were assembled together, one of the company made some remarks which he did not approve, and he rebuked him with so much violence and harshness, that another minister present begged him to stop, saying: 'Why, brother, if you attempt to correct a person for the most trifling fault, you take a sledge-hammer and beat his brains out.' But this is a kind of help no one likes to receive.

I was reading lately an account of the very kind way in which a gentleman belonging to the Society of Friends once helped a man who had injured him. He was a preacher among the Friends, but a tanner by trade, and known to all as one 'who walked humbly with his God.' One night a quantity of hides were stolen from his tannery, and he had reason to believe the thief was a quarrelsome, drunken neighbour whom we may call John Smith.

The next week the following advertisement appeared in the county newspaper :—

'Whoever stole a quantity of hides on the fifth of the present month, is hereby informed that the owner has a sincere wish to be his friend. If poverty tempted him to this false step, the owner will keep the whole transaction secret, and will gladly put him in the way of obtaining money by means more likely to bring him peace of mind.'

When the thief read this advertisement, his heart was quite subdued, and he felt very sorrowful. A few nights afterwards, as the tanner's family were about retiring to rest, they heard a timid knock, and when the door was opened, there stood John Smith with a load of hides on his shoulder. Without looking up, he said, 'I have brought these back, Mr. Savery; where shall I put them?'

'Wait till I can get a lantern, and I will go to the barn with thee,' he replied; 'then, perhaps thou wilt come in and tell me how this happened. We will see what can be done for thee.'

While they were gone, his wife prepared some hot coffee, and placed other refreshments on the table. When they returned from the barn, she said, 'Neighbour Smith, I thought some hot supper would be good for thee.'

He turned his back towards her and did not speak. After a few moments, he said, in a choked voice, 'It is the first time I ever stole anything, and I have felt very bad about it. I am sure I didn't think once that I should ever come to what I am. But I took to drinking —then to quarrelling. Since I began to go down hill, everybody gives me a kick. You are the first man that has offered me a helping hand. My wife is sick, and my children are starving. You have sent them many a meal, —God bless you,—and yet I stole the hides. But I tell you the truth when I say it is the first time I was ever a thief.'

'Let it be the last,' replied William Savery; 'the secret still remains between ourselves. Thou art still young, and it is in thy power to make up lost time. Promise me that thou wilt not drink any intoxicating liquor for a year, and I will employ thee to-morrow on good wages. Thy little boy can pick up stones. But eat a bit now, and drink some hot coffee. Perhaps it will keep thee from craving anything stronger to-night. Doubtless thou wilt find it hard to abstain at first; but keep up a brave heart for the sake of thy wife and children, and it will soon become easy. When thou hast need of coffee, tell Mary, and she will always give it thee.'

The poor fellow tried to eat and drink, but the food seemed to choke him. After vainly trying to compose his feelings, he bowed his head on the table and wept. After a while, he ate and drank, and his host parted with him for the night with the friendly words, 'Try to do well, John, and thou wilt always find a friend in me.'

He entered into his employment the next day, and remained with him many years, a sober, honest, and faithful man.

Now this is an instance of help rendered with great kindness; and if we desire to help any one, we must always try to do it in a kind way. This is what Jesus does. He is always kind, 'even to the unthankful and to the evil.'

On one occasion, while Jesus was on earth, the Pharisees brought to him a woman who had been guilty of a great sin. They wanted Him to say that she ought to be stoned to death. Jesus said, 'Let him that is without sin among you cast the first stone at her.' Their consciences told them that they were all sinners; and they went out, one by one, till 'Jesus was left alone, and the woman standing in the midst. And He said unto her, Hath no man condemned thee? She said, No man, Lord. And Jesus said unto her, Neither do I condemn thee. Go, and sin no more.'

And in that dark hour before Jesus was delivered to the Jews to be crucified, when His heart was sad and sorrowful, He took His disciples into the Garden of Gethsemane, and desired them to watch while He went a little way from them to pray. When He returned, He found them sleeping. Many persons would have reproached them for what looked like ingratitude and want of kind feeling, but Jesus only said: 'What, could ye not watch with me one hour?'

Jesus tells us in the Bible that He 'will not break the bruised reed, nor quench the smoking flax.' He compares Himself to a good shepherd, 'who carries the lambs in His bosom,' and gently folds them in His arms. The help He gave to those who sought it when He was on earth was always kindly given.

If any came to Him for instruction, He taught them kindly, never upbraiding them for their ignorance and dulness. If any came with their troubles and afflictions, He sympathized with them and helped them.

He gave health to the sick—sight to the blind—hearing to the deaf—strength to the feeble—comfort to the sorrowing—life to the dead. And what He gave was always given with kind, gentle, loving words. If any came confessing their sins, He received them graciously, and forgave them tenderly. And even when reproof and rebuke were necessary, 'the law of kindness still dwelt upon His tongue.'

And He is the same now as when in love and in meekness He moved among men. He is still always *near to help, always able, always willing*, and *always kind in helping*. These are the four reasons why Jesus is THE BEST HELPER.

My dear children and friends, let us seek the help of Jesus. We all need it in everything we have to do. We need it in all the engagements and occupations of daily life; but most especially do we need it in the important business of seeking our soul's salvation.

Ah! let us all begin *to-day*, and ask help from Jesus. He is ready to give it if we pray to Him for it. He has power enough and love enough to grant all we need.

And let us try to imitate our blessed Saviour. Let us seek His grace to make us like Him in helping one another. We cannot, like Jesus, be *always near*, nor are we *always able* to help; but we can be like Him in being *always willing* and *always kind*, and in seeking in every way to do good to our fellow-creatures.

> 'To do His Heavenly Father's will
>   Was His employment and delight;
>   Humility and holy zeal
>   Shone through His life divinely bright.
>
> 'Oh, how benevolent and kind,
>   How mild, how ready to forgive!
> Be this the temper of our mind,
>   And these the rules by which we live.
>
> 'Dispensing good where'er He came,
>   The labours of His life were love;
> Then, if we bear the Saviour's name,
>   By His example let us move.'

THE END.

SGCB Titles for the Young

Solid Ground Christian Books is honored to be able to offer over a dozen uncovered treasure for children and young people.

Bible Warnings: *Sermons to Children on Dangers that lie along their Path and How to Avoid Them* by Richard Newton is the sequel to *Bible Promises* that you hold in your hand. Fifteen brilliant chapters. Newton at his very best!

Bible Promises: *Sermons to Children on God's Word as our Solid Rock* by Richard Newton directs children to rest in the certain promises of God.

Heroes of the Reformation by Richard Newton is a unique volume that introduces children and young people to the leading figures and incidents of the Reformation. Spurgeon called him, *"The Prince of preachers to the young."*

Heroes of the Early Church by Richard Newton is the sequel to the above-named volume. The very last book Newton wrote introduces all the leading figures of the early church with lessons to be learned from each figure.

The King's Highway: *Ten Commandments to the Young* by Richard Newton is a volume of Newton's sermons to children. Highly recommended!

The Life of Jesus Christ for the Young by Richard Newton is a double volume set that traces the Gospel from Genesis 3:15 to the Ascension of our Lord and the outpouring of His Spirit on the Day of Pentecost. Excellent!

The Child's Book on the Fall by Thomas H. Gallaudet is a simple and practical exposition of the Fall of man into sin, and his only hope of salvation.

The Child's Book on Repentance by Thomas H. Gallaudet is a simple and practical exposition of the Fall of man into sin, and his only hope of salvation.

The Child's Book on the Soul by Thomas H. Gallaudet is a simple and practical exposition of the Fall of man into sin, and his only hope of salvation.

The Child at Home by John S.C. Abbott is the sequel to his popular book *The Mother at Home*. A must read for children and their parents.

My Brother's Keeper: *Letters to a Younger Brother* by J.W. Alexander contains the actual letters Alexander sent to his ten year old brother.

The Scripture Guide by J.W. Alexander is filled with page after page of information on getting the most from our Bibles. Invaluable!

Feed My Lambs: *Lectures to Children* by John Todd is drawn from actual sermons preached in Philadelphia, PA and Pittsfield, MA to the children of the church, one Sunday each month. A pure gold-mine of instruction.

Truth Made Simple: *The Attributes of God for Children* by John Todd was intended to be a miniature Systematic Theology for children. Richard Newton said that Dr. Todd taught him how to teach children. Practical and crystal clear!

The Young Lady's Guide by Harvey Newcomb will speak directly to the heart of the young women who desire to serve Christ with all their being.

The Chief End of Man by John Hall is an exposition and application of the first question of the Westminster Shorter Catechism. Full of rich illustrations.

Call us Toll Free at 1-877-666-9469
Send us an e-mail at sgcb@charter.net
Visit us on line at solid-ground-books.com

www.ingramcontent.com/pod-product-compliance
Lightning Source LLC
Chambersburg PA
CBHW022133080426
42734CB00006B/342